# Look, Duck & Vanish

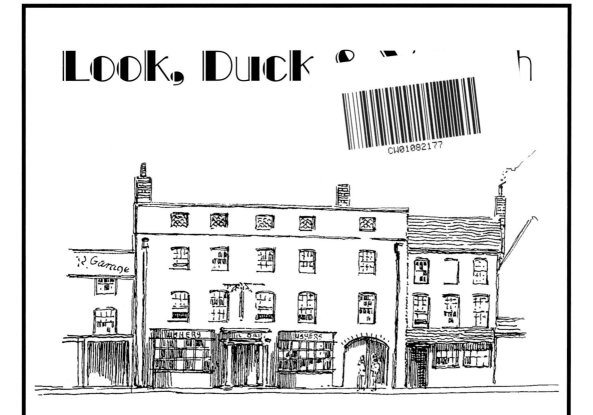

CW01082177

## A history of the 6th (Marlborough) Battalion
## Wiltshire Home Guard
## 1940 - 1944

# ROGER DAY

Published by ROGER DAY,
77 Chilton Way,
Hungerford, Berkshire, RG17 0JF

**Web Site: www.ramsburyatwar.com
Email: roger@ramsburyatwar.com**

Copyright Roger Day, 2011.

All rights reserved. No reproduction, copy or transmission of this publication may be made
without written permission.

Any person who does any unauthorised act in relation to this publication may be liable to
criminal prosecution and civil claims for damages.

First published 2011.


ISBN 0 9536601 4 1

Printed by Synergie, Newbury, Berkshire, RG14 5TU

Design and Cartography; Roger and Christopher Day.

The authors and publishers have made every effort to trace copyright holders, but if they
have inadvertently overlooked any, they will be pleased to make the necessary arrangements
at the first opportunity.

*Previous page:* Throughout the unit's existence the Royal Oak in Marlborough High Street
served as battalion HQs. This pen and ink drawing of the establishment appeared on a
souvenir card that was signed by many of the battalion's officers. Unfortunately the artist's
identity is unknown. The card was presented to Lt. Col. Fuller, the battalion's first
commander, on the occasion of his farewell dinner on 8th March 1943. (Mrs 'Vee' Fraser)

# Table of contents

## *Preface and acknowledgements*

Although I have always been interested in the Home Guard, until recently the thought of writing a book on the subject never crossed my mind. That all changed during the spring of 2008 when Sir Sydney Giffard made contact asking if I would be interested in some documents relating to the Marlborough Home Guard. They had belonged to his father, Walter Giffard, who had served throughout the war as both Marlborough's 'B' Company and later battalion commander. I was very excited at the prospect of seeing this material and we arranged a meeting. The detail and range of documents Sir Sidney entrusted into my care was beyond my wildest dreams and I quickly made up my mind to study and record the history of the 6th (Marlborough) Battalion, Wiltshire Home Guard - this book is the product of that research.

My greatest concern, as I embarked on the project, was that I had left things too late and would struggle to find anyone living with first hand accounts of the Home Guard. Fortunately, to my great relief, I was wrong and have managed to find and interview over twenty veterans who served for varying periods of time in the Marlborough Battalion. Sadly, some of those interviewed have since passed away, which fills me with great sadness, as they never got to see their stories in print.

I have found a substantial amount of information relating to the battalion's history in files held at the National Archives, London; Wiltshire and Swindon History Centre, Chippenham; Marlborough College Archives; Marlborough Library; Wiltshire Heritage Museum Archive and Library (for kindly allowing me permission to use the extract on page 48 from the William Young Diaries) and the Alexander Keiller Museum, National Trust, Avebury.

I would also like to take this opportunity to thank the following individuals: Will Bennett, John Bower, Ron Bridges, Ray Brooks, Ray Beasley, 'Dickie' Brown, George Cady, Dr. Rosamund Cleal (Curator, Alexander Keiller Museum, National Trust, Avebury), Miss Murial Cobern, Mark Clements, Clifford Cowles, Joe Crook, Bob Curnick, John Day, Roland and Margaret Day, Albert Dean, Andrew Deane, Mrs Vonnie Dickens, Don Dobson, Tony and Joan Dobson, Bill Eastmond, Rodney Farley, Bruce Fox, Mrs 'Vee' Fraser, Iain Fry, William Gauntlett, Sir Sydney Giffard, Mrs Sylvia Gilbert, Terry Heard (Archivist, City of London School), Harold Herring, Tony Honeyman, Roger Hues, Ken Hulbert, George Johnson, Eric Jones, Nigel Kerton (Wiltshire Gazette and Herald), George Lanfear, Colin Lee, Ron Liddiard, Keith Light, Derek Looney, 'Mac' McKechnie, Murray Maclean, Chris Martin, Peter May, Richard Metters, Dan Miles, Roger Miles, Hugh Mulligan (609 [WR] Sqd. Association), Graham Palmer, Heather Peak-Garland, Mrs Brenda Pearce, Roger and Audrey Peck, Reg Perry, Peter Piper, Rodney Priddle, Len Richardson, Brian Rickards, John Robins, Dr. Terry Rogers (Archivist, Marlborough College), Maura and Harry Sheppard, David Sherratt, Mrs Carol Silk, David Smith, Steve Smith, Mrs Mary Spender, Gordon Starling, Mrs Wendy Stevens, Andrew Tilley, Bob Townsend, 'Tiny' Watts, John Wilson, Bob Wise, Mrs Kathy Withers, Eddy Witts and Peter Woodford. I must also thank my wife Sandra and son Christopher for their help and encouragement. If I have inadvertently overlooked anybody please accept my sincere apologies.

Finally, my interest in the 6th Marlborough Battalion does not end with the publication of this book, as I am fairly certain there's a lot of material still waiting to be rediscovered. I therefore invite any reader with further information to please make contact, so that it might be included in future editions of 'Look, Duck and Vanish'.

Roger Day
Hungerford, Berkshire, October 2011

# Introduction

During the spring of 1939, with war clouds gathering, Britain, France and Poland agreed to support each other should they be attacked by Nazi Germany. On 1st September Adolf Hitler invaded Poland and the following day Britain and France issued ultimatums demanding that Germany withdraw or face war. When the British ultimatum expired at 11am on Sunday 3rd September no word had been received from Hitler's government, and fifteen minutes later Prime Minister Neville Chamberlain reluctantly declared war on Germany. Almost immediately a British Expeditionary Force (BEF) was dispatched to France, but it was too little too late and 28 days later Poland fell.

Many had expected the Germans to continue their offensive and push westwards, but instead there followed a period of inactivity - on land at least - which became known as 'The Phoney War'. This state of affairs continued for just over six months until 9th April 1940 when Hitler launched an attack on Denmark and Norway. Just over one month later, on 10th May, the British and French armies were taken completely by surprise when German armoured units, part of Army Group A, bypassed the Maginot Line and pushed westwards at amazing speed through the Ardennes region of Belgium - an area of dense forest which the allies considered unsuitable terrain for tanks. At the same time Army Group B, which was largely made up of infantry units, launched an attack towards Rotterdam and Antwerp. Supporting the armour and infantry were dive-bombers, paratroopers and gliders. This tactic, based on speed and surprise, was called 'Blitzkrieg' (meaning lightening war) and the Germans quickly pushed the allied armies back towards the channel ports.

Meanwhile, back at home the British people were becoming increasingly worried by the news. Fears of an invasion rapidly began to increase and concern grew that German paratroopers would be dropped all across Britain to join forces with a 'fifth column' - a term used to describe a clandestine group of people whose aim was to undermine a nation from within. During the early months of WWII many people believed that such a column was already operating in Britain, and although these stories had no firm base, the seed of doubt had been sown and the government soon found itself under pressure to intern all aliens with German or Austrian backgrounds. Equally worrying was the very real prospect of civilians forming their own private little armies and the government decided to act quickly before things got completely out of hand.

Meanwhile the war situation on the Continent was worsening with every passing day and British and French troops now found themselves cut-off and surrounded - their only means of escape was via the beaches and port at Dunkirk. Between the 24th May and 4th June over 338,000 allied soldiers were evacuated from the port in an operation codenamed 'Dynamo'. Winston Churchill heralded the evacuation as a 'miracle of deliverance' but warned the country not to look upon it as a victory by adding 'wars are not won by evacuations'. However it was a great boost to British moral, but there was no way of hiding the fact that this had been the worst defeat suffered by the British army in its long history. Over 68,000 soldiers were killed, missing or taken prisoner and 2,500 guns, 74,000 vehicles, 20,000 motor cycles, 77,000 tons of ammunition, 416,000 tons of supplies and 165,000 tons of petrol had been left behind.

On 22nd June 1940 France surrendered to Germany leaving Britain alone to face the might of Hitler's all conquering military juggernaut. In a speech made in the House of Commons on 18th June Churchill, who on 10th May had succeeded Chamberlain as Prime Minister said, *"What General Weygand called the Battle of France is over. I expect that the Battle of Britain is about to begin"*.

It was within this climate that the Local Defence Volunteers (LDV) - later, at Churchill's suggestion, re-named the Home Guard - was born, a force that would eventually grow into the largest unpaid army ever raised in Britain. The account that follows is the history of one small part of that organisation - the 6th (Marlborough) Battalion, Wiltshire Home Guard.

# 1. The anti-parashooters

Within days of Churchill forming his new government the pace began to quicken and at a War Office meeting held on 12th May the need for some kind of Home Defence Force was hastily agreed. The following day all the essential details were worked out and on the evening of Tuesday 14th May, during the BBC's nine o'clock news, the Secretary of State for War, Anthony Eden, made a radio broadcast to the nation announcing the formation of the LDV.

Earlier that same day the Home Office sent a telegram to the chief constables of every police force in Britain. It read, *"Broadcast will be made at 9:10pm today inviting male British subjects between the ages of 17 and 65 to register for Local Defence Volunteer Corps against enemy landing by parachute or otherwise. Registration will be at any police station. Circular follows. In meantime please ensure forthwith that all stations are prepared to receive registrations. Following particulars should be taken in each case viz. name, address, age, whether familiar with firearms, present occupation, any previous military experience and whether prepared to serve away from their homes"*.

In the circular that followed it was stressed that the police were not going to be permanently responsible for the control or administration of the LDV. The reason why police stations were initially chosen as places to enrol potential volunteers was because nearly every town and village had one and each station would be able to provide all the necessary facilities. A supply of forms for recording details of each volunteer arrived at Wiltshire's Police Headquarters in Devizes on the day of Eden's broadcast, and quantities were immediately distributed to all the counties police stations and houses in anticipation of the expected rush of volunteers. It is not clear from the above what forms had been issued, but the following is an extract from a memo sent by Marlborough's LDV commander on 25th June, which leaves the author in little doubt that Army Form W3066 was the document in question. *'Most important that all men accepted for duty with LDV should be formerly enrolled and accepted for service on form AF W3066 and...all men already enrolled to date have in fact been formally enrolled on AF W3066'*.

On 17th May a memo was sent out to all Wiltshire Police Districts, of which Marlborough was one, asking how many volunteers had registered in each section and to provide a list of those who it was felt had suitable qualities to become area, zone or group organisers. At a local level it was Britain's Lord Lieutenants who were called upon to get the ball rolling and interview suitable candidates for the top jobs. The Lord Lieutenant of Wiltshire was Sir Ernest Wills from Littlecote who in company with Noel Llewellyn, Wiltshire's Chief Police Constable, approached General Sir John Francis Gathorne-Hardy GCB GCVO of Lockeridge House and asked him if would accept the post of Area Organiser for Wiltshire - he eagerly accepted the challenge. During the First World War he had been a General Staff Officer, serving in Italy and on the Western Front, and between 1933 and 1937 was Commander-in-Chief at Aldershot.

Nationally, within the first five days of Eden's appeal over 250,000 men had volunteered to join the new force, and the totals for Marlborough's seven sections were as follows:

| | |
|---|---|
| Marlborough section | 192 |
| Ramsbury section | 50 |
| Netheravon section | 45 |
| Pewsey section | 64 |
| Beckhampton section | 17 |
| Ludgershall section | 71 |
| Great Bedwyn section | 84 |

Two of the first to enrol in Marlborough were Dickie Brown and his father who both lived in the tiny hamlet of Durley on the southern edge of Savernake forest. *"After the appeal my father, who had served in the First World War, said 'Well, I'm game for it' and I said 'yes, let me come along'. Mum wasn't very keen, but we both went to Marlborough Police Station and I think we were among the first half dozen to join".*

Eddy Witts lived in a thatched cottage in Lucky Lane on the eastern side of the village of Mildenhall (pronounced Minal). *"I can remember quite distinctly Anthony Eden doing his radio broadcast. I was working for Wiltshire County Council and was in the surveyor's department at Pewsey at the time and used to cycle there and back each day. He [Eden] said that anyone who was interested and over the age of 17 should report to a police station. So the following evening, on my way home from work, I went round to Marlborough's Station in George Lane, but they [the officers on duty] knew nothing about it! Anyway they took my name and address and a few weeks later I went out on my first patrol".*

Don Dobson from Marlborough was an early volunteer and remembers his first night on duty. *"You must understand that no one really seemed to be in charge of anything. We assembled on Marlborough Common more or less opposite the cemetery. Some people had shot guns but all I had was my Boy Scout knife, as I was only 16 at the time. We decided to wander off in pairs over Rough Down, which had been ploughed up to grow food. Christopher's cottage was on the edge of the common then and we patrolled all around there - in the beginning we quite expected the Germans to drop parachutists".*

The government had promised the new force weapons and uniforms, but the BEF had left so much material behind in France that most of the remaining equipment in Britain was being issued to the regular army. Therefore, on 16th May a radio broadcast was made asking for owners of rifles to loan them to the LDV. However, a week later, despite the apparent shortages, an official consignment of rifles, ammunition, caps and overalls left the Ordnance Depot, Tidworth, destined for 13 different locations throughout Wiltshire. One of the locations was the armoury at Marlborough College, which received 100 rifles, 1,000 rounds of ammunition, 200 caps and 150 overalls. The limited numbers meant that only a few rifles could be made available for each platoon and on Wednesday 5th June Captain Giffard, the Beckhampton section organiser, delivered three .303 Short Lee Enfield rifles and 30 rounds of ammunition to William Young, who was in charge of the Avebury platoon - the previous day Young had also taken delivery of four uniforms.

On 24th June the responsibility for organising Wiltshire's LDV was taken away from the police and given to the county's Territorial Army Association, which no longer had a full time role to play following the army's mobilization in 1939 - its vacant offices and drill halls would make ideal quarters for the embryonic LDV. The association's staffing levels had been reduced and in Wiltshire there was just a secretary, assistant secretary and a clerk, but as the workload of looking after the LDV became more demanding, so their numbers increased.

By the end of July 1940 the county of Wiltshire had been divided into 8 LDV Battalions. At that time Marlborough's area coincided with the Marlborough Police District, which included Pewsey, and was known as the Marlborough and Pewsey Battalion LDV. In charge, as well as being Wiltshire's area organiser was General Gathorne-Hardy. His Aide-de-Camp (ADC) was Mr J H Clay and the Royal Oak in the High Street became the Battalion's HQ.

**Above left:** General Sir John Francis Gathorne-Hardy. (via Sir Sydney Giffard)
**Above right:** Captain Loraine Fuller, Marlborough's first battalion commander. (Mrs 'Vee' Fraser)
**Below:** Members of Marlborough's 'A' Company pictured at a Sunday parade during the late summer of 1940. Addressing the gathering is General Gathorne-Hardy and standing slightly behind and to his left is Captain Fuller. (Mrs 'Vee' Fraser)

The battalion was then sub-divided into two half battalions and in command of the Marlborough Half Battalion was Captain Arthur Loraine Claude Fuller - known to family and friends as 'Rainie'. During the First World War he had served with the 6th Dragoon Guards (Carabiniers) but was now working as the estate manager for Sir Ernest Wills at Littlecote and was a very good organiser. It may have been his employer, in his capacity as Lord Lieutenant of Wiltshire, who encouraged 'Rainie' to take on the very demanding job of running the Marlborough Half Battalion. He lived with his wife and two children in a large house on the edge of Savernake forest called Furze Coppice, which belonged to the Ailesbury estate and had once been a hunting lodge. On 19th May his wife made the following entry in her diary. *"'Rainie' out all day having been given command of this area for the 'anti-parashooters' - fearful organisation to get going"*. During the early days of its existence the press had dubbed the LDV 'parashooters' or 'parashootists', as they thought their main role was to shoot German paratroopers as they descended - fortunately neither of the names caught on. However, the press interpretation was fundamentally correct and to emphasise the point, and legalise the corps, Sir Percy Grigg, the under-secretary of state for war, made a statement in the House of Commons on 22nd May in which he said, *"They [the LDV] are wanted to deal with the action of small enemy parties landed from the air. We had seen what the effects of this landing of small numbers of troops from the air had been in other countries and it was important to organise means of local action against the measures which small parties landed in various places might take. The volunteers are also wanted for the purpose of observation and information of landings."*

It was not long before Marlborough and Pewsey were made full battalions in their own right. The Marlborough Battalion boundary encompassed the old Marlborough and Ramsbury Rural District, together with the parish of Burbage and the Borough of Marlborough. Its command structure, as of 23rd July 1940, was as follows:

### Marlborough LDV Battalion
Commander - Captain A L C Fuller

### Marlborough Borough Area Company
Commander - T C G Sandford Esq

No. 1 City of London Staff Platoon - Captain Workman
No. 2 City of London Boys Platoon - Major Henderson
No. 3 College Boys Platoon - Major Harling
No. 4 Salisbury Road Platoon - W D Clayton Esq
No. 5 London Road Platoon - W E Lawrence Esq
No. 6 Mildenhall Road Platoon - J D Siddall Esq
No. 7 Swindon Road Platoon - J H Parmenter Esq

### Beckhampton Area Company
Commander - Captain W Giffard

No. 1 Ogbourne Platoon - H Godfrey Esq
No. 2 West Overton Platoon - L Ross Esq
No. 3 Broad Hinton Platoon - Austen Horton Esq

### Ramsbury Area Company
Commander - Captain W Brown
No. 1 Ramsbury Platoon - E Wilson Esq
No. 2 Aldbourne Platoon - Major S Bland
No. 3 Baydon Platoon - Col. Board
No. 4 Chilton Foliat and Froxfield Platoon - H J Skinner Esq

### Bedwyn Area Company
Commander - Col. S H Thunder

No. 1 Great Bedwyn Platoon - E R Pole Esq
No. 1a Durley Observation Post and Patrol - L Wootton Esq
No. 2 Burbage Platoon - B Ford Esq
No. 3 Shalbourne Platoon - T Burgess Esq
No. 4 Buttermere and Ham Platoon - J Macpherson Esq
No. 5 Wilton Platoon - R W Margesson Esq
No. 6 Fosbury Platoon - Sir Eastman Bell
No. 7 Little Bedwyn and Chisbury Platoon - E Gauntlett Esq

### The Rootes' Estate (Stype Grange)
Commander - J C Rankin Esq

No. 1 Stype Grange Platoon - J Gifford Esq

In the early days of the LDV the organisation had no proper rank structure, as the War Office refused to grant military status to civilians. However, retired officers who joined the LDV liked to be known by their old military titles, and those serving in the Marlborough Battalion were no exception, as can be seen in the table above.

The idea that the LDV should have no rank structure was all well and good, but someone had to be in charge of each unit, and it was important those under command could quickly and easily recognise who it was. On 24th June the following list of 'positions' and their respective distinguishing marks was issued:

| | |
|---|---|
| Zone Commander | 4 stripes |
| Battalion Commander | 3 stripes |
| Company Commander | 2 stripes |
| Platoon Commander | 1 stripe |

The stripes were made of braid and were to be worn on both shoulders. The only NCO rank at this stage was for section commanders who were instructed to wear Sergeants stripes, usually on the left sleeve only.

In February 1941, to improve the Home Guard's discipline and efficiency, the use of the army's rank structure was granted, and it worked as follows: Battalion Commander - Lieutenant Colonel; Company Commander - Major; Platoon commander - Captain or Lieutenant; Section Commander - Sergeant; Squad Commander - Corporal or Lance Corporal.

**Left and centre left:** When war broke out, Marlborough's future Home Guard Commander, 'Rainie' Fuller, was enjoying a family holiday near Salcombe, Devon aboard his motor yacht 'Bluebird'. (The boat had been constructed in 1931 for the world's land and water speed record holder Sir Malcolm Campbell). In May 1940 she was requisitioned by the Admiralty and became one of the 'little ships' used during the Dunkirk evacuation.

**Bottom:** 'Rainie' lived on the edge of Savernake forest in a property called Furze Coppice, which belonged to the Ailesbury estate. Its beautiful gardens were his pride and joy. **Below right:** The huge crater left by a German bomb dropped somewhere in the forest during August 1940. (All pictures Mrs 'Vee' Fraser)

# Marlborough Home Guard Battalion map showing company and platoon areas

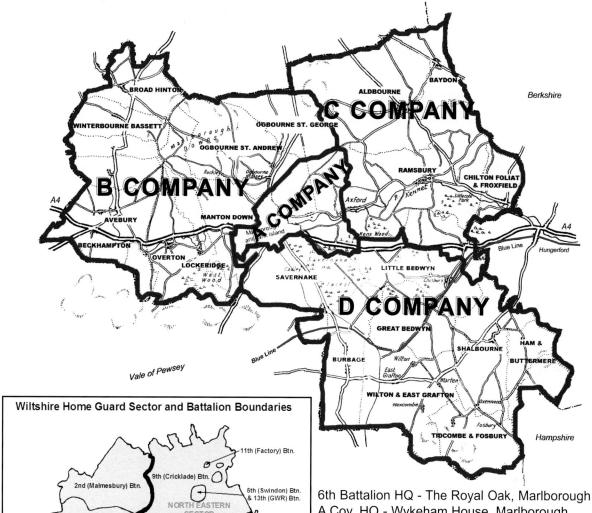

6th Battalion HQ - The Royal Oak, Marlborough
A Coy. HQ - Wykeham House, Marlborough
B Coy. HQ - Lockeridge
C Coy. HQ - Aldbourne
D Coy. HQ - Shalbourne, later moving to Wilton

By early 1942 'A' Company had grown considerably in size and a decision was made to split it in two and create 'E' Company. This new company included all of the Marlborough College and CLS Platoons, a platoon of Post Office employees, the transport platoon and the town's air raid wardens. (The wardens had formed their own Home Guard Platoon to help strengthen the defences of the anti-tank island) 'E' Company was commanded by Major Orton with Lt. William Harling as his 2nd in command. 'A' Company moved its HQs to Wye House with 'E' Company taking over at Wykeham House.

# 2. Getting organised

## Observation posts

Tommy Trinder, a well known stand-up comedian of the time, told his audiences that the letters LDV stood for Look, Duck and Vanish. In reality his comic interpretation was surprisingly accurate, as the authorities saw observation, rather than confrontation, as the force's principle role. However, the Wiltshire Area Commander's orders of July 1940 were slightly at odds with those of his masters in Whitehall, stating that as soon as the enemy appeared the LDV's duties were 'to watch him, hamper him and eventually destroy him'.

To help in this task a network of observation posts (OPs) was quickly established across the entire country. From these OPs patrols kept a lookout for the first signs of invasion, rapidly passing anything of interest to the appropriate authorities. Every night on the downs around Marlborough men from each platoon (normally four in number) manned their posts from dusk until dawn taking regular turns to go out on duty. Old iron wheeled shepherd's huts belonging to local farmers provided many of the patrols with shelter, and tractors or horses were used to haul them to suitable hilltop locations across the region.

William Gauntlett was in charge of the Little Bedwyn Platoon and recalls, *"We had an old corrugated iron shepherd's hut to the north of Chisbury camp. Being on duty was quite good on clear moonlight nights. The great difficulty was keeping awake in the warmth after a hard days work".*

Audrey Peck (nee Mundy) grew up in Lockeridge during the war and her father was in the local Home Guard platoon. *"I used to stand in the window of our house and watch him go on duty up the hill past Fyfield to the shepherd's hut. I used to cry because I didn't want him to go - the house felt empty without him there. One story he told us, which always made us laugh, was when he was on duty one night with a chap called 'Curly' Staplehorn. In the middle of the night 'Curly' woke my father and said 'Fred I can hear a noise like someone coughing'. Dad went through the procedure of shouting 'Halt, who goes there?' and heard a noise that sounded like a stifled cough. Then, out from the undergrowth came a Hedgehog".*

Bob Curnick, who served in the Ogbourne St Andrew platoon throughout the war, remembers their OP was near Four Mile Clump, a plantation of trees on the Marlborough Downs four miles north of the town. *"We did shifts of four hours on and four hours off. There was an old shepherd's hut equipped with two palliasses for the two off duty watchmen. The palliasses were soon infected with fleas, so I preferred to sleep in my car, or on a nice summer night on the grass. It was fascinating to hear the owls and see the dim light of the glow-worms".* Throughout the summer and early autumn of 1940 men from the Ogbourne St Andrew Platoon, in common with most platoons across Britain, spent the nights manning their OP looking out for German gliders or airborne troops. During the winter months the post was relocated to the saddle room of a disused stables near Ogbourne Maisey.

Not all the OPs were old shepherd's huts. During early July 1940 Avebury's platoon used a cart to carry sections of curved corrugated sheeting up to their patrol post on the Ridgeway. The sheets were bolted together to form a very basic shelter known as an 'elephant hut'.

Len Richardson was a private in Baydon's Platoon and their OP was on Peaks Down, which is one of the highest points in Wiltshire with panoramic views over large parts of the Marlborough and Lambourn Downs. *"We had an old chicken house up at Peaks. The first time we used it we were all bitten by fleas! One night I was up there on duty with Bill Habgood who was a bit of a timid bloke. The moon was shining beautifully, it was frosty and we were on guard by the beech trees. I heard a crunch, crunch, crunch, noise coming up through the trees. I said to Bill 'Look out, here they come!' and as the noise got closer Bill took to his heels and ran like hell! I knew all along what the sound was - it was a badger creeping through all the leaves".*

Overton Platoon had their OP on Wyman's Hill and at first used a shepherd's hut for shelter. A wooden shed later replaced this, but unfortunately it only lasted a short time before it was destroyed during a violent storm.

The arrival of autumn gales signalled an end to all thoughts of a German invasion in 1940 and the hilltop OPs were left unmanned until the following spring. On 16th March 1941 William Young decided to inspect post 'E', as Home Guard commanders had received orders to re-commence night OP duties at the end of the month. The post was situated on the Ridgeway and reached from Avebury via Green Street. As Young made his way towards the downs he was shocked to find that the track way had been cut up by tanks and lorries during a recent army exercise and was only passable by foot.

Some members of Young's platoon had requested that a heater should be made available to those on night duty, as they found the 'elephant hut' a cold place to sleep. Young responded to their demands and arranged for a shepherd's hut, complete with stove, to be pulled up to the post by tractor. The move took place on Saturday March 29th, but unfortunately there had been more army manoeuvres during the previous week, plus heavy rain, which meant the track was in an even worst condition than it had been two weeks earlier! Nevertheless, after much skidding and sliding in the mud the hut was eventually hauled up to the highest part of the Ridgeway to become the new centrally heated post 'E'.

Despite this success Young was still worried by the poor condition of the track, as in his opinion it would considerably hinder the passing of messages from the post to platoon HQs in Avebury. Because of his concerns he was successful in persuading his company commander to allow him permission to move the post to Windmill Hill.

## Roadblocks

Manning roadblocks was one of the LDV's main duties. Unfortunately, the over zealous way in which some members carried out their orders made them very unpopular with road users. Clifford Cowles, whose father Tom was in the Aldbourne Platoon, remembers one such incident. *"Mr McKeon was in charge of my father's section and they were patrolling the Lodge road out of Aldbourne. One evening the officer in charge of the POW camp at Baydon came along in his car, but wouldn't stop at their check point, so they shot his tyres out - he had to stop then! Nobody got into trouble, everything was sorted out and they never heard anymore about it".*

Eddy Witts remembers manning a roadblock on the Ramsbury road just outside Marlborough near Poulton. *"Mr Siddall, who lived in a bungalow just beyond the railway bridge at Poulton, was the Sergeant in charge. We had a couple of bell tents in the field on the left just after you cross the river going towards Minal. We spent two hours on and two hours off duty and tried to get some sleep in the tents. We were mostly young lads armed with 12 and 16 bore shot guns and had great fun when the girls we knew went by. We would ask them who they were and demand to see their identity cards! The check point was right on top of the bridge, but there was no barricade so we just used to stand in the road and wait."*

As the months passed so the roadblock at Poulton was improved slightly, as John Bower recalls. *"We used to stand guard at the bottom of Poulton hill and had barbed wire, which we pulled across* the road to form a roadblock. We had to stop everybody who passed. I knew most of the people who lived in Minal, but I still had to challenge them with 'Halt, who goes there?' and they had to stop and show me their identity cards". Another volunteer who regularly found himself on duty at the Poulton roadblock was Don Dobson. "We did come across some well known Marlborough figures who were out with other well known people's wives. We just pulled the barricade back and said 'Pass friend'".

Dickie Brown from Durley often found himself on duty at Durley gate with Lionel Wootton. "Because I was the boy of the outfit they used to put me on duty with Lionel. He was head keeper for the Savernake Estate and had been in the army during the Boer and First World Wars, reaching the rank of Sgt. Major. The incident I remember the best concerns some horse slaughterers from Milton Lilbourne. They used to send a lorry up to London every night loaded with meat - God knows what they did with it! Because of the smell you didn't want to be the one to have to challenge them at the Durley roadblock. During the early hours of one morning I was on duty when their lorry arrived at the block on its way back from London. I stepped out into the road and the lorry stopped. Sitting by the driver was this young soldier. I'd seen the driver many times before and didn't bother to ask for his identity card, but I did asked the soldier if I could see his pay book. He replied 'I'm not giving my pay book to toy soldiers'. I said 'you must' but he still refused, so I shouted 'Lionel, trouble'. Lionel came out looking every bit the Sgt. Major and said 'pay book lad' to which the soldier replied 'I've already said I'm not handing my pay book over to toy soldiers'. 'Please yourself' said Lionel 'I'm going to count to three - doubt whether you'll hear three. One, two...'don't shoot, don't shoot, said the soldier and quickly handed his pay book over. Lionel looked at the book and said 'don't you try that again my boy, in another two seconds you could have been dead. After they had gone I said to Lionel 'would you have really shot him?' and he said 'too true I would. I've shot bigger buggers than that for breakfast!'

George Cady remembers an incident that occurred in Burbage. "The Burbage LDV set up a roadblock consisting of two old farm carts by Seymore pond, just on the road to East Grafton. One Friday evening they let the local butcher through the block to deliver his meat to customers in East Grafton. For some reason when he returned to Burbage they refused to let him back through. The situation became very heated and the village policeman was called out to defuse the incident!"

Early in the war George Edwards was on duty at a roadblock in Ramsbury during a joint ARP, Home Guard and Fire Service exercise. "I let a man through my roadblock without checking his identity card. I'd known the man all my life but I was reprimanded and told that he might have been a German spy or Fifth Columnist!"

Soon the emphasis started to change and some of the men were taken off roadblock duty and given other tasks. "The next big worry was that the Germans would drop parachutists on water works or sewage farms", recalls Don Dobson. "So we left our barricade at Poulton and went to guard the water works near the railway station and the sewage farm in Elcot Lane - it was thought the Germans would contaminate the water and muck up the sewage. We guarded these places every other night and sheltered in the work's buildings where we used to clean our rifles. One idiot accidentally fired his rifle and the bullet whizzed around the concrete walls of the building! During the early hours of one morning I was on guard at the water works. It had rained hard the previous day and the water was dripping off the leaves. You could get very frightened being on guard alone and the noise the dripping water made on the gravel drive sounded like somebody walking along".

## Stop lines

Before Germany launched its campaigns against Norway and the Low Countries the only invasion defences Britain had were leftovers from previous conflicts, and apart from plans to protect its major seaports very little thought had been given to improving the situation. However, as soon as Germany started to demonstrate its new 'Blitzkrieg' tactics Britain was forced to consider ways of protecting itself from a possible Nazi invasion.

At the beginning of 1940 the Commander-in-Chief Home Forces was General Kirke, but on 27th May he was replaced by General Edmund 'Tiny' Ironside who was given the responsibility of devising a plan for defence of the United Kingdom. On 5th June Ironside held a meeting in London of the LDV and leading members of the force from all across the country were invited to attend. Captain 'Rainie' Fuller, Marlborough's newly appointed battalion commander, went along. Ironside's address was quite lengthy but included some very practical advice. The audience was told that he wanted them to develop the 'Molotov Cocktail', which had been used so successfully in Finland against the Russians. He then went on to stress the importance of static defence and promised that all members of the LDV would eventually be equipped with weapons and uniforms. Occasionally his tone was quite belligerent and when speaking on the subject of parachutists he said, *"…when they come down, you can shoot them, shoot them, shoot them without any reference to taking any kind of care of their future"*. It's difficult to tell how much Ironside's talk inspired those present, but on his return to Marlborough 'Rainie' Fuller immediately went out with his wife to inspect roadblocks.

Because so much military equipment had been left behind in France Ironside had little choice but to rely on static defences such as pillboxes, anti-tank ditches, roadblocks and minefields, and in June 1940 construction began on the largest single military defence programme ever undertaken in Britain.

Starting at the coast and then moving inland Ironside created a series of stop lines using, wherever possible, existing features such as canals, rivers and railway lines, which would act as anti-tank barriers. It was hoped that each stop line would delay an invading force long enough for troops held in reserve to rush forward and counter-attack. In addition a number of important communication centres were turned into anti-tank islands, a subject that will be dealt with in more detail later.

The only stop line passing through the Marlborough Home Guard Battalion area followed the course of the Kennett and Avon canal and was known as the General Headquarters (GHQ) line. It was the backbone of Ironside's defence plan and stretched from Bristol across southern England to Maidstone where it turned north passing to the east of London and then on towards the Wash - the section through Wiltshire was known as the Blue Line. It entered the Marlborough area at Savernake and then passed through the parishes of Burbage, East Grafton, Great Bedwyn, Little Bedwyn and Froxfield before leaving the area at the Berkshire county boundary. Home Guard detachments from each of the six places mentioned would have been responsible for manning their section of the line in the event of an invasion.

On 19th July, less than two months after his appointment, Churchill ordered Ironside to retire from his post and the following day General Alan Brooke took command. Churchill felt that his generals lacked imagination and that their doctrine was based too much on the static battles fought during WWI. Brooke had been a corps commander with the BEF in France and Belgium and when the German offensive began he distinguished himself well. He witnessed at first hand how Germany's 'Blitzkrieg' tactics worked and believed in a more fluid approach to defence strategy - shortly after his appointment as C-in-C Home Forces things began to change.

On 14th August orders were received to stop further new work on all stop lines. However, nearly all the permanent defences along the entire length of the Blue Line, from Bradford-on-Avon to Tilehurst, had been completed and on 12th September work started on an interim report outlining their uses and identifying problem areas. It included such things as, camouflaging pillboxes, sighting additional posts and making arrangements for the manning of the line by the Home Guard.

The report also highlighted a number of worrying problems with the line; *"The canal cannot be called a satisfactory obstacle for various reasons. It is, in fact, in certain places, hardly an obstacle at all. The locks present special difficulties. If the gates are destroyed the water may sink to such a level above them as to leave the canal bottom dry. Again the large beams on the gates are themselves ideal for bridging while the locks are only some 15ft across with firm banks".*

*"There are many bridges of all sorts. The permanent ones have been prepared to receive 'asparagus' [vertical steel rails placed in concrete sockets] but in my opinion on the wrong [or enemy] side where they are difficult or almost impossible to cover with fire. Swing bridges have been provided with a jamming arrangement, but as far as I am able to ascertain no bridge in the whole Blue Line has been prepared for demolition".*

Brigadier Studd, who was responsible for the Wiltshire section of the Blue Line, also picked up on the poor sighting of roadblocks on canal bridges. He had identified nine places where roadblocks had been sited on the enemy side of humpbacked bridges and where it would be impossible to cover these by fire, allowing enemy troops to pull out the rails with ease. To solve this problem he asked for, and was granted, permission to build additional roadblocks on the opposite or friendly side of the nine bridges in question.

## Defended towns and villages

To deny the enemy freedom of movement over territory sandwiched between each stop line Ironside's plan included the establishment of a network of defended towns and villages. It was hoped that the locations chosen would delay the enemy's progress long enough for reinforcements to arrive. The places selected in the Marlborough area were the villages of Aldbourne, Chilton Foliat, Ogbourne St George, Avebury, Broad Hinton, Beckhampton, Great Bedwyn, Burbage and Bagshot, plus the town of Marlborough.

At first sight the decision to defend Bagshot, a small hamlet two miles south of Hungerford, may seem a little odd. However, near Bagshot is Stype Grange and during the war it was the home of William Rootes whose family owned some of Britain's major car companies such as Singer, Humber and Hillman. When war broke out their factories started building vehicles for all of Britain's armed forces, as well as aircraft - one out of every seven bombers produced during the war was manufactured by the Rootes Group. The group's headquarters was Devonshire House, a massive mansion block opposite the Ritz Hotel in Piccadilly, London and when war broke out the HQs was evacuated to Stype Grange. Because of its importance and size it formed its own LDV unit and plans were drawn up to defend the Bagshot area in the event of an invasion. Little is known about this unit, but its existence appears to have been short lived, as by 1941 the responsibility of defending the area seems to have passed to the Shalbourne Home Guard Platoon.

With the exception of Bagshot most of the villages were centred around road junctions and the principle aim was not to defend the settlement, but to prevent the enemy free passage through it. Roadblocks were constructed on the main routes leading in and out, but they had to be temporary in nature, so as not to hinder the movement of any counter-attacking force. Many blocks consisted of rolls of concertina barbed wire laid out in a 'U' shape with the open ends facing the enemy. Mines were also to be laid and covered with straw. If at all possible the roadblocks were sited with houses on both sides from which members of the LDV could throw Molotov bombs onto any tanks disabled by the mines. Each position was to be covered by one or two rifle posts. Unfortunately the plan was dependant on the provision of mines, which were in very short supply during the summer of 1940! On Saturday 6th July work started in Avebury on this type of barricade when a squad of regular soldiers arrived by truck from Tidworth. The blocks were sited so that they could be thrown across the four roads leading into the village at a moments notice.

Other blocks that were considered effective against wheeled vehicles were put together using farm carts, agricultural machinery and old motor vehicles. It was important that one element of the block was moveable so that a gap could be left, which would be plugged in the

S T Y P E.

D PRECAUTIONS.
INSTRUCTIONS.

of Civil Defence depends here, as
upon voluntary service for the
quired. Everyone

| | | |
|---|---|---|
| Fire Posts. | Locations and Personnel as Lists attached. | Air Raid Wardens will, during their initial patrol, endeavour to assist in preparing, ready for immediate use, equipment at various posts. |
| Despatch Riders. | From Shelter Personnel. | Of two motor cycles always kept ready for immediate use in the garage, upon sounding of alarm, one is to be taken to the New Garage. Whoever is detailed for the duty will collect his mount from most convenient point. |
| Telephone | | It will be the responsibility of the Telephone Operator in charge of the Board, to switch No.201 Hungerford through to Mr.Gifford's Office (L.D.V.Section Post) and test line between switchboard and office before proceeding to Shelter. |
| L.D.V.Platoon Commander - Mr.Rankin | | who will issue all L.D.V. instructions, but whenever daytime Air Raid Alarm is sounded, the succeeding night's patrol must immediately report to Section Post, don uniforms and await further orders. The Patrol leader will |

-11-

This twelve page document was published on 31st July 1940 at the Stype estate and given to estate workers and Roote's Group employees. It contained important contact information and telephone numbers plus useful instructions on all aspects of air raid precautions, including, fire, first aid, air raid shelters, gas and unexploded bombs. On page 11 mention was made of the group's LDV unit and that Mr Rankin, the platoon's commander, was responsible for issuing all LDV instructions. On the following page it made clear that the use of firearms was restricted solely to members of the LDV. The office of Mr J Gifford, who appears to have been the estate manager at the time, was used by the platoon as a section post - it was occupied continuously 24 hours-a-day.

The fact that work of national importance was taking place at Stype is exemplified by the paragraph on page four entitled 'Instructions to Telephone Operators' - *Our telephone number has been included in the priority system to receive warning messages by telephone. We shall only receive, however, one warning, which means that an air raid may occur in five to ten minutes. This is the warning upon which a public warning signal is sounded and executive action with regard to air raid precautions taken.*

event of an invasion. Such a block, made from bits of ancient wheeled agricultural machinery laid out to form a chicane, was established on the A4 just to the west of Marlborough near the Cotton and Littlefield college houses.

## Marlborough anti-tank island

The defence of Marlborough was slightly more complicated, as it had a duel role to play. Like the villages it was defended by the LDV, but in the event of an invasion alert would receive assistance from a detachment of regular troops (comprising 8 officers and 200 men) who would be transported to the town in buses from Tidworth. Initially they would defend Marlborough in exactly the same way as the villages, but in the later stages of its defence would turn it into a 'tank island'. The town's transformation required the construction of fixed defences such as pillboxes, anti-tank blocks and gun emplacements at entry points all around the borough. Should the Germans break through the Blue Line it was hoped the troops in Marlborough would attack their flanks as they passed by and slow their advance northwards.

**Above:** An illustration from Military Training Pamphlet No. 30, Part III: Obstacles, showing the best method of using coils of barbed wire for roadblocks. It was important to site the block near a bend so that it was encountered unexpectedly.

**Right:** Portable knife rests were made from angle iron, brushwood poles or square timber and were suitable for blocking gaps that needed to be opened on a regular basis. Neither of the obstacles illustrated here would have been much good at stopping tanks.

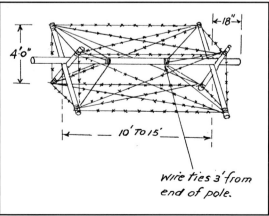

During May 1940 the Marlborough College Officer Training Corps was asked to form an LDV unit. It was open to all boys who were 17 or older, but in order to join they had to get permission in writing from their parents. John Wilson, who had been a student at Marlborough College since 1936, was one of the unit's first members and recalls the arrival in Marlborough of a small party of Royal Engineers led by a Captain. *"They arrived one Wednesday afternoon in June to make some form of elementary defences and I and another boy were attached to the OC for local knowledge and sandbag filling duties. The only defence positions I can remember being involved in was loop holing and sandbagging what is now the upper floor of the garage of The Hermitage to provide firing positions covering Hyde Lane to the north"*.

During the war years Keith Light from Overton was a pupil at Marlborough Grammar School and every day on his way to and from school passed through a roadblock on the A4 sited below the college bridge. *"There was a machine gun and sandbags up in the window on the bridge facing west. There was a turret in the bricked up bay window of Mount House and a pillbox by the college facing the bridge"*.

On Saturday 17th August Captain 'Rainie' Fuller's 11-year-old daughter, 'Vee' (now Mrs 'Vee' Fraser) spent part of the day making dozens of 'bombs' from sawdust wrapped in newspaper in preparation for a mock battle that was to take place in Marlborough the following day. *"I remember they looked like things you see in a cartoon. The next day we were on the bridge that goes over the A4 at the college throwing these 'bombs' onto tanks as they came through"*.

At the end of July temporary roadblocks, made from rolls of barbed wire, old vehicles and knife rest barriers, had been positioned around the town, but these would eventually be replaced by more substantial anti-tank roadblocks once the decision was made on where best to locate them. The new blocks consisted of bent rails and concrete cylinders or 'pimples' covered by fire from fixed anti-tank weapon positions and machine gun posts. As soon as the most suitable sites were chosen construction work went out to contract.

For safety reasons, where roadblocks encroached onto the carriageway, white guide lines had to be painted on the road surface and the blocks illuminated at night using lamps. Despite these precautions the positioning and layout of some roadblocks still caused serious problems and several accidents, including three fatalities, occurred at the roadblock near St Peter's church on the A4 at Marlborough. It was stated in a letter dated 22nd October 1941 that the accidents were caused by the presence of two concrete cylinders on the footway, which presumably forced pedestrians to walk out onto the busy carriageway to avoid them. The letter was written by the Divisional Road Engineer who suggested removal of the offending obstacles.

To prevent German pilots using Marlborough's white horse as a navigational aid it was camouflaged by the Ministry of Home Security, but details of exactly how the chalk figure was disguised have not been recorded. Others in the region were painted green, but after heavy rain the paint washed off and the work had to be done again.

Mention should also be made at this point about rail blocks. There were two sites on the railway track to the south and south-east of the town - one near the London Road bridge (A4) and another on the main running line near the high level goods yard. From careful study of wartime aerial photographs it seems they consisted of lengths of slotted precast concrete laid under the rails between the sleepers. In the event of 'Action Stations' hairpin rails, identical to those used at roadblocks, would have been dropped into the slots by the Home Guard. Small concrete cylinders may then have been rolled or lifted into position to act as additional obstacles.

The railway tunnel, just south of the town, was also guarded, as George Johnson recalls. *"There were normally about 10 men on duty at any one time with two standing guard at each end of the tunnel. Also at each end were bell tents provided for those who were not on guard. The older men often played cards, but one night they couldn't find a candle to light the tent, so Sgt. Jack Wiltshire and myself walked through the tunnel and borrowed a candle from the tent at the other end!"*

# Change of plan

By March 1941 the emphasis had changed dramatically from those proposed by Ironside ten months earlier. Stop lines no longer formed part of the overall plan because General Alan Brooke considered them to be out of place in modern warfare. Instead a series of strong points, or centres of resistance - in essence an improvement on the already established principle of defended towns and villages - was brought into being. In future the only places on the Blue Line that were to be manned were those adjacent to settlements, such as Great Bedwyn, where the local Home Guard could make use of the line's pillboxes and other strong points to defend the village.

Many of the Blue Line's redundant defences, such as concertina barbed wire, bent rails and 'asparagus' were taken and reused elsewhere to strengthen the defences of places like Marlborough. On 9th April Brigadier Studd wrote to HQs Southern Command on this subject and part of his letter read:

*"Now that the 'GHQ Stop Line' defence is abolished, in so far as Wiltshire is concerned, there are a large number of bent rails and 'Asparagus' on these lines which will not be required for defence purposes in the 'Defended Locality' Scheme on which I am now working. When my Defended Locality Scheme is perfected it would enhance it enormously if certain localities astride the main communications could be provided with proper anti-tank stops".*

On 2nd July 1941, possibly as a direct result of this memo, the doubling of sockets and rails in North Wilts District commenced. The work started in Marlborough and the process continued until all blocks in the district had been dealt with.

At this stage it's interesting to note that the confusing names attached to defended towns and villages, such as, strong points, centres of resistance and defended localities were gradually renamed 'Tank Islands' and placed into three categories (A, B, & C). Prior to this change there had only been three tank islands in Wiltshire - Swindon, Marlborough and Salisbury - now there were 11 in category 'A' and 25 in category 'B'. Marlborough was classified in the first category whilst Avebury, Ramsbury, Chilton Foliat and Ogbourne St George fell into the second. The designation 'Category A' meant the entire town was tank proof whilst 'Category B' meant just a small area of the town, called the 'keep', was tank proof. However, it is not clear what 'Category C' was, or if any of Marlborough's villages were included in it!

The term 'Vulnerable Point' was still in use but now described a specific site of importance and the only example in the area was Marlborough's Telephone Repeater Station on the London Road. Post Office personnel, plus a resident police officer, were responsible for its protection between 6am and 11pm with a detachment from the town's Home Guard covering the remaining period.

By 1941 most of Marlborough's defences had been completed and the map on the following page lists the various types and marks their positions around the town. Reproduced on pages 26 to 30 are period and modern photographs showing some of the defended locations. To help illustrate what was taking place in the surrounding villages during the same period, the map on page 31 shows the plan to defend Chilton Foliat from the south and east.

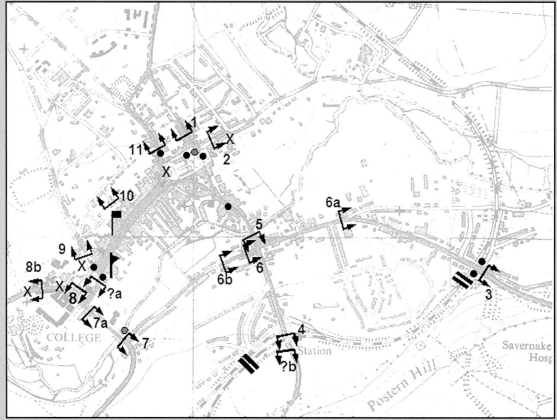

# The Marlborough anti-tank island - 1942

Most of the roadblocks are labelled using the original wartime numbering system. However, a question mark has been used for blocks, which for reasons best known to the wartime planners, were never allocated numbers. (Reproduced from First Series 1:25,000 Ordnance Survey maps. With the kind permission of the Ordnance Survey)

**Key:**
- ● = Pillbox Round
- ⌐⌐ = Roadblock
- X = Strong Point
- Γ = Battalion HQ
- ⊢ = 'A' Coy. HQ
- ⬡ = Pillbox Hexagonal
- ≡ = Rail Block

1 - Herd St 12 rails
2 - Mildenhall Rd 10 rails
3 - Hungerford Rd 14 rails
4 - Burbage Rd 12 rails
5 - Gasworks Bdg 12 rails
6 - George Ln (east) 10 rails
6a - Roebuck Inn 22 rails
6b - George Ln (west) 10 rails
7 - Cowbridge 15 rails
7a - Pewsey road 14 rails
8 - Church west corner 6 rails
8b - Fyfield Road 16 rails
9 - Hyde Lane 8 rails
10 - Lane off High St 8 rails
11 - Kingsbury St 10 rails
?a - Church east corner 10 rails
?b - Track to signal box 18 RSJs 8x6

# Defending Marlborough

**Left:** Just a tiny selection of the bewildering choice of official and commercially produced training publications available to the Home Guard.

**Above:** The Home Guard Signals Room in the Royal Oak sketched by a College boy. Arthur Pepin was a Master at the College, as well as the battalion's communications officer, and College boys frequently manned the room. (Marlborough College Archives)

# Defending Marlborough

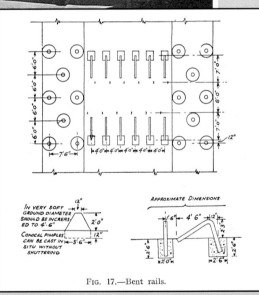

FIG. 17.—Bent rails.

**Above:** This 1943 picture shows the lower part of Kingsbury Street, Marlborough, looking south. Clearly visible on each pavement either side of the road are two concrete pimples. Careful inspection shows that embedded in the road between the obstacles are a number of sockets, which were made from short lengths of pipe set in concrete, the top being flush with the road surface. When not in use the sockets were plugged. However, in the event of 'Action Stations' the plugs were removed and bent rails, which can be seen leaning against the wall behind the two pimples on the left, were slotted in place (see diagram on right reproduced from Military Training Pamphlet No. 30 Part III: Obstacles). It was thought that if an enemy tank attempted to charge this type of block the bent rail would provide an incline that would raise the front of the tank and expose its less well protected underside to anti-tank fire. Just beyond the rails, partially hidden by a picket fence, is a small pillbox and behind the men crossing the road are two loopholes disguised to look like windows. (Reproduced by permission of English Heritage. NMR)

**Right:** The Kingsbury Street pillbox is one of only two in Marlborough that have survived to the present day (2011).

# *Defending Marlborough*

**Top:** The north facing ground floor wall of Dormy House, which is on the corner of Silverless Street and Kingsbury Street, was reinforced with concrete and turned into a strong point. Its two loopholes were disguised to look like windows and designed to cover the Kingsbury Street roadblock with protective rifle and machine gun fire. Dormy House is behind the two men crossing the road in the picture at the top of the previous page. (Reproduced by permission of English Heritage. NMR)

***Above left and right:*** After the war the loopholes were bricked up, but despite the passage of more than seventy years the inside wall has changed little, and the loophole positions and thick concrete are still clearly evident. (With thanks to Shield Management Services)

# *Defending Marlborough*

*Above:* The area around The Green was heavily defended. There were anti-tank roadblocks in Herd Street and St Martins plus a strong point opposite the junction of Blowhorn Street. Three pillboxes were erected on The Green and one (a type 25) is visible centre right. An hexagonal pillbox (possibly a type 24) was built at the junction of Herd Street and Silverless Street and a further type 25 positioned a few yards to the west beside the British restaurant.

*Below:* Two type 25 pillboxes were constructed at the western end of the High Street and both are visible in this picture. The example on the left was on the pavement outside Wykeham House and had a false sloping roof and imitation windows painted on its walls. The other box was directly opposite on the pavement beside the Sun public house and disguised to look like an extension of the building. (Both pictures reproduced by permission of English Heritage. NMR)

# *Defending Marlborough*

**Above:** In June 1940 John Wilson was a student at Marlborough College and helped a party of Royal Engineers cut a loophole on the upper floor of the garage belonging to The Hermitage in Hyde Lane. The hole was designed as a firing position to cover the Hyde Lane roadblock and survives to this day (see also left)

NO PARKING

**Right:** This picture was taken in June 1943 during a joint British and American exercise codenamed 'Columbus'. The tank is a British Covenanter and it has just turned left out of George Lane onto the Pewsey Road. In the background is Cow Bridge and just to the right of the tank, partially hidden behind a picket fence, is Cow Bridge pillbox. Also of interest is the concrete cone (one of four) and sockets in the road, clues to the exact position of Marlborough's No.7 roadblock. (British Pathe Ltd)

# Defending Marlborough

**Above:** The college arch over the A4 at the western edge of the town. Beyond the arch, in the centre of the picture, is Mount House, which had its northern ground floor window converted into a gun emplacement. An anti-tank roadblock crossed the A4 at a point near the car on the left and the bridge and wall on the left would have been ideal places for members of the Home Guard to ambush enemy tanks.

**Above:** There was once a doorway in this flint wall. During the war the opening was fortified and cleverly disguised as a wooden door. The window of the door was really a loophole for a machine gun to help protect the High Street should an attack come from the west.

**Right:** The door can just be seen behind the soldier on the right in this group of American paratroopers, who were pictured in the graveyard of St Peter's Church during the summer of 1944. (Harold Stedman)

# Defending Chilton Foliat

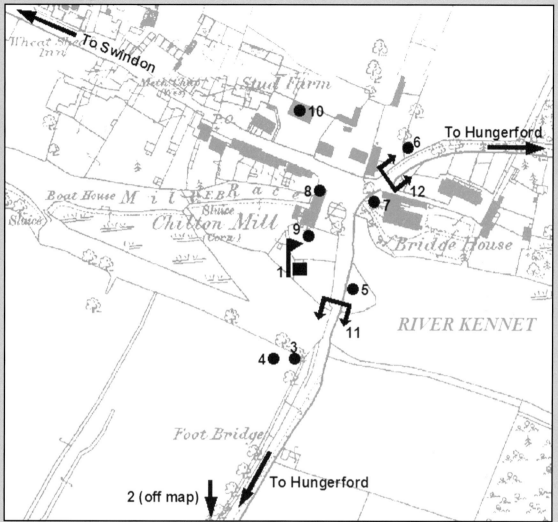

**Home Guard plan to defend Chilton Foliat from the south and east - 1942**

Based on wartime aerial photographs, information held at the Swindon and Wiltshire Record Office and the memories of the late Mr Ray Brooks.

## Key:
**1** - Platoon HQs (Riverside Cottage) Lt Skinner, sergeant and three men
**2** - Skeates corner - bombing post (3 men)
**3** - Glebe Meadow - Spigot mortar (5 men)
**4** - Glebe meadow - Lewis MG (4 men)
**5** - Bombing pit in woodland north-east of bridge
**6** - Allotment path - Spigot mortar (5 men)
**7** - Bridge House wall - weapons pit (5 men)
**8** - Chilton Mill - sniper's post (4 men)
**9** - Mill House lawn (4 men)
**10** - Baverstock's Barn (12 men)
**11** - Kennet Bridge roadblock - 16 rails
**12** - Bridge House roadblock - 14 rails

# *Defending Chilton Foliat*

**Above:** Riverside Cottage was the home of Chilton Foliat's Home Guard Commander, Lt. Jack Skinner.
**Right:** A wartime picture looking north across the Kennet bridge. A roadblock, consisting of 16 bent rails (also known as hairpins), crossed the road at the point where the railings on the right meet the bridge parapet. (Francis Becker)
**Below:** A section through a roadblock showing how the rails slotted into the road - the sloping portion faced away from the centre of the block towards the enemy.

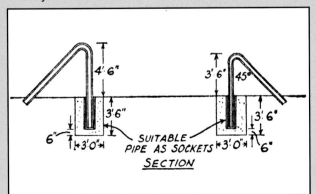

4' 6"    3' 6"   45°

3' 6"     3' 6"

6"   3' 0"    SUITABLE PIPE AS SOCKETS   3' 0"   6"

SECTION

# 3. Dodging the bombs

Wiltshire is one of southern England's least populated counties, so it comes as a bit of a surprise to discover just how many bombs were dropped on the region during the war. The highest concentration occurred during the latter half of 1940. Most fell harmlessly on open countryside and were probably dropped by aircraft that had been damaged by anti-aircraft fire, intercepted by fighters or simply lost their way. Unfortunately time and space prevents me from recording them all here, so the following is just a selection of the more noteworthy events.

The first record of bombs dropping in the Marlborough area occurred at Overton Hill on the night of Friday 9th August 1940. In my view this is one of the best-documented accounts of any bombing event I have ever read. The following has been extracted from an account sent by William Young, Avebury's Platoon Commander, to Walter Giffard who was in charge of the Beckhampton Company. Before the war Young had been the principle archaeologist working for Alexander Keiller on the excavations at Avebury, which may explain the very precise nature of the report.

*"On returning to Avebury at 9 o'clock (having been to Marlborough for rifle practice) I went on OP duty on the Ridgeway with A Tucker, R Huntley and E Cook. We drove up to the post in a lorry. A Tucker and myself were on duty for the first period, up till one o'clock. Captain Giffard visited us at half past ten, while we were having a belated supper, which we had not had time to eat before.*

*About eleven o'clock, as we were patrolling southwards, we heard what we thought to be an enemy plane passing overhead from the direction of Pewsey Vale. Searchlights were apparently endeavouring to locate it from the direction of Knapp Hill. The plane passed directly over us, and it seemed to be following the line of the Ridgeway. Suddenly we saw three quick flashes beyond the northern end of the ridge, but heard no report of any kind. This might be accounted for by the fact that there was a strong southerly wind blowing at the time. At the same moment the plane was heard to wheel left and it immediately turned back, presumably following the Swindon-Avebury road. On reaching Avebury it bore towards the south-east and crossed over the Ridgeway above the large bell barrow in the third clump of trees from our patrol post. At a point about 110 yards north-west of the barrow, it dropped a high explosive bomb on the open down just above a rectangular earthwork in the valley, which is shown on the 6 inch Ordnance Map. Directly afterwards a second bomb dropped on the berm of the barrow, on the north-western side of the tree-covered mound. The plane then made for the direction of Overton.*

*Guided by the sound, we were looking towards the course it was taking, and so witnessed the incident quite clearly from slightly higher ground. We heard the whizzing sound of the bombs as they fell and saw them burst. It was almost like a fireworks' display, the bursting fragments spreading upwards in the air some thirty feet or so. I counted four seconds between the time we saw the exploding bombs and the spot where they fell. At the time, however, we could not be absolutely certain of the position, but only knew the direction, and thought that they might have fallen anywhere beyond Kennett for that matter.*

*Shortly after 12 o'clock we heard voices in the direction of West Kennett, and then saw red lights flashing about on the down. One of the lights then approached our part of the Ridgeway, and we heard people whistling to one another. This made us suspect parachutists. When the light came within halting range, I challenged the bearer of it three times, but received no audible reply, and Arthur got ready to fire.*

*To give him a fourth chance I then bawled 'halt' once more as loudly as I could, and asked him why the hell he did not reply to our challenge. Only then did a voice reply, 'Alright; it's only the police!' Out of the darkness loomed a lumbering, bulky figure, panting and blowing and wearing a steel helmet. It was PC Furse of Overton, and he explained that he had not heard us on account of the strong wind... All I can say is that he was very lucky, particularly as Arthur, who had been bored and peevish lately, as nothing exciting had occurred, was simply dying for the chance of having a shot at somebody just then. From one or two remarks, which he dropped later, I gather that he was extremely disappointed at missing this grand opportunity of having a pot shot at a copper! The rest of the night was uneventful.*

*On leaving our OP at 5 o'clock the next morning, we drove southwards along the down in the lorry to look for any signs there might be of the raid. After searching the area around the first two clumps of trees that disfigure prehistoric burial mounds, we were hailed from the other side of the combe by Sergeant Fox and PC Furse, who had found the crater made by the second bomb, and were standing by it. Mr Osmond, Chief Air Raid Warden, and Mrs Osmond were with them. They had not found the crater made by the first bomb, but when we got there and had pointed out the direction of the spot where we saw it fall, Mr Osmond climbed on top of the lorry and from this vantage point he spotted the crater about 110 yards further north-west. The craters were no more that three feet in depth and about four feet in diameter at the bottom. Each was, however, 12 feet across the top".*

Three weeks later, during the night of 28th/29th August, seventeen high explosive bombs fell in the Marlborough area and several exploded near Winterbourne Bassett, as Ron Bridges recalls. *"I was visiting my future wife at her parent's home when the bombs dropped. They fell near Richardson's cottages, which were about a mile away. The explosions blew barbed wire fences up into the trees and the craters were eight to ten feet deep".* Ron thinks the Germans were trying to hit Yatesbury Camp and was later told that Arthur Watts, who lived in Richardson's Cottages, may have inadvertently attracted their attention when he went outside, because he forgot to shut his door or switch the light off! The blast blew the doors off his cottage and threw him back into the house.

## Invasion scare

Those who found themselves regularly patrolling the downs around Marlborough during the long hot summer of 1940 must have often wondered, as they gazed out across the tranquil Wiltshire countryside, what the future held in store. Night duty, especially for farmers who had already put in a strenuous full days work in the harvest fields was a lonely tiresome business, and their imaginations often went into overdrive. Sights and sounds so familiar in daytime took on a different meaning as darkness fell - the dim light from glow-worms or the sound of moving animals could easily be misconstrued as signalling fifth columnists or the stealthy approach of enemy troops. Nevertheless those on duty had every reason to feel apprehensive, as the prospect of a German invasion of Britain during that first summer of the war was very real indeed.

By the end of June the Germans had started drawing up plans for an invasion of the British Isles, which they codenamed 'Operation Sealion'. For the plans to succeed it was vital the Luftwaffe gain control of the skies over Britain by destroying the Royal Air Force. The airborne assault started on Tuesday 13th August with RAF airfields and the Chain Home radar stations the principle targets - the main seaborne landings were expected to take place three or four weeks later. The best conditions of moon and tide favoured a landing sometime between 6th and 10th September. Throughout the week leading up to this period British intelligence had noticed a substantial build-up of invasion barges at ports along the channel coast between Ostend and Le Havre, and the general feeling was that an invasion was not too far off. Desperate times demanded desperate measures and at the end of August a memo was received at Marlborough Home Guard HQs from Tidworth Garrison stating that in the event of an invasion petrol pumps were to be put out of action - the supply was to be contaminated by adding water. George Cady was the Durley section's dispatch rider and was given the job of contaminating the petrol. *"They gave me a ration of sugar and the keys to the petrol tanks of the two garages in Burbage - Central and Seymore. If there was a German landing my job was to go and unlock the tanks and drop sugar into the petrol so that the advancing enemy army could not use it. - I never used any in my tea!"* (Sugar in petrol can cause all sorts of problems, as the petrol becomes very sticky and clogs up the filter, pump and carburettor starving the engine of fuel and causing a stall).

On Saturday 7th September the Luftwaffe launched what turned out to be the most ambitious operation it ever directed against the British Isles. So much importance was placed upon its success that Reichsmarschall Hermann Goring, the Luftwaffe's titular head, travelled by train to the Pas de Calais in order to personally supervise the day's events. Late that afternoon he stood on the cliffs at Cap Gris Nez and watched wave upon wave of fighters and bombers head towards London. It was the greatest aerial armada yet seen with nearly 1,000 aircraft taking part.

As the bombs descended upon London the city began to burn, but it was the docks and warehouses of the East End that suffered most and a huge black cloud, fed by thousands of fires, towered above the area blocking out the late afternoon sun. Unfortunately London's ordeal had only just begun because shortly after 8:00pm, and guided by the fires on the ground, small groups of bombers, part of a second wave, began to approach from the Thames estuary. In total a further 318 aircraft bombed London over a period of eight-hours, and it was not until 4:30 the following morning that the all clear was sounded.

As the day's events were still unfolding the Chiefs of Staff met at 5:20pm to discuss the massive raid's implications. If, in their opinion, the perceived threat of invasion had increased, there were three levels of alert available to them:

Invasion Alert No. 3 - an attack is probable within three days.
Invasion Alert No. 2 - an attack is probable within two days.
Invasion Alert No. 1 - an attack is imminent.

At 8:07pm the Chiefs of Staff issued Invasion Alert No. 1 - this was signified by the announcement of codeword 'Cromwell'. Fifty minutes later the message was received at HQs Salisbury Plain Area and a further codeword, 'Resolute' (meaning 'Action Stations') was immediately sent out to all concerned. On receipt of 'Resolute' Wiltshire's District Commanders passed the message to every unit under their command, including all Home Guard Battalions. Within three hours vulnerable points had been reinforced, tank island garrisons sent out and the Home Guard's OPs, Road Blocks and other defences fully manned.

Throughout the afternoon and evening most of Britain had gone about its normal business blissfully unaware of the terrible events taking place in London. William Young, Avebury's platoon commander, arrived back in the village at about 9:30pm following an enjoyable day out, and went to bed. At a quarter-past-midnight he was woken by a telephone call from Captain Giffard who told him the OP on the Ridgeway was to be manned day and night until further notice. Young immediately went up to the post and told the men on duty there to be on the alert, as an invasion might be expected at any moment.

Baydon, at just over 750 feet above sea level, is Wiltshire's highest village and in order to maintain constant water pressure has its supply fed from a tower that stands beside Finches Lane. The present tower was built in the 1970s but it replaced an earlier concrete structure dating from the mid 1930s. The Baydon Home Guard used the tower as an OP and during the invasion scare Rowland Day was manning the post. As he looked to the east he could see a tremendous glow lighting up the horizon that looked like a spectacular sunrise, and correctly guessed that London was being hit.

Don Dobson lived near the junction of Herd Street and Blowhorn Street in Marlborough and was a member of Sgt. Pearce's section. On the night in question he was fast asleep in bed and recalls, *"I was woken by dad who came into the bedroom shouting 'can't you hear? Sgt. Pearce is down there knocking the door down. He wants you to go outside with your gun because the Germans are coming and he wants you to drive them off!' We had a sandbagged emplacement at the junction so we could control traffic coming along the Swindon road. It was about 2 o'clock in the morning and I went out to the position and waited there until eventually some of our chaps came by in a lorry, and I found out it had all been a false alarm".*

By dawn on September 8th it was clear the Germans had no immediate plans to invade. At 8:30am Salisbury Plain Area ordered the Tank Island Garrisons to return to barracks and the Home Guard was stood down from its defences. However, as a precautionary measure all OPs continued to be manned until the morning of 10th September.

Britain had survived its first major invasion scare of the war, and although reports from other parts of the country suggested that issuing codeword 'Cromwell' had caused confusion and panic, this does not appear to have been the case in Wiltshire, as everything went very much according to plan.

## Home Guard under attack

On the morning of Sunday 27th October 1940 several hundred men, drawn from all corners of the Marlborough Home Guard Battalion area, assembled on Manton Down to watch a demonstration by the RAF.

Prior to the exercise men from the Marlborough Company marched through the streets of the town behind the band before heading to the display area via Kingsbury Street. Troops from the battalion's other three companies arrived in buses and lorries provided by the Royal Army Service Corps, and were dropped off in groups near the common. The men then formed up into their individual platoons before marching off towards the spot where the demonstration was to take place. Surprisingly, local people were allowed to watch the display and hundreds turned up to take advantage of the free show.

A Captain Williams provided commentary via a loudspeaker and at exactly eleven o'clock a signal flare was fired and the demonstration began. The object of the exercise was to familiarise the Home Guard with tactics being used by the Luftwaffe against allied ground troops. Three aircraft, a Westland Lysander, Bristol Blenheim and Fairy Battle took part and initially they made three flypasts in line astern at 2,000, 1,000 and 500 feet respectively. At 11:10am there was a short talk about gas and then the commentator sounded a warning rattle. This was the signal for everybody to put on their gas masks in preparation for the next part of the exercise where all three aircraft sprayed liquid over the troops to represent a gas attack. Dive-bombing and low level sweeps followed with the planes making clever use of the folds in the ground allowing them to sneak up at head height and take everybody by surprise.

The last item on the programme, timed for 11:50am, was listed as, 'dive attack and aerobatics by Hurricanes'. 'Eddy' Witts was one of those taking part in the exercise and recalls, *"We had been watching the RAF display when suddenly the planes disappeared and we waited expectantly for something new to arrive. A few minutes passed and then somebody shouted 'there it is!' A plane was approaching from the southeast at between 1,500 and 2,000 feet. It flew over Granham Hill and the college before circling north towards Ogbourne. I recognised it as a German bomber - it was a twin-engine job, a Dornier I think, and it was the first time I'd seen a German plane. It then disappeared from view for a minute or two before re-appearing over Marlborough heading west. It then dropped two bombs, which exploded about half-a-mile away near the Devil's Den. Nobody had any ammunition and we were all told to scatter. A little while later the Lysander returned and dropped a message attached to a bit of red tape. I watched it come fluttering down - it was a warning note telling us a German plane was coming!"*

George Johnson was too young to be actively involved but was one of the many civilians who had made their way to the edge of the exercise area to watch. *"It was the chance of seeing aircraft that was the attraction - we hadn't seen many before the war! All of a sudden a German plane came over. I'm not sure what type it was, but it had two engines. I actually saw the bombs going down and they landed near the Devil's Den. That night on the radio 'Lord Haw Haw'* [see page 43] *announced that the Germans had bombed the Home Guard!"*

Sydney Giffard, whose father was in command of the Beckhampton Company, was also watching the demonstration. He recalls, *"My impression was that the German unloaded his bombs hurriedly and uselessly, because he was suddenly aware of RAF aircraft close to him - his bombs knocked over a number of fat sheep, who had to be helped back onto their hooves afterwards - I was told it was a Heinkel 111".*

Bob Wise was a member of the Overton Home Guard Platoon, but until the enemy plane's unscheduled appearance he'd not been paying much attention to what was happening. *"Nobody took much notice until a couple of ruddy bombs dropped out of it. We didn't know what was going on and just gawped at them until they hit the ground. You never saw so much panic in your life - the blokes didn't know where to run because there was no cover! Afterwards everybody treated the incident as a bit of a joke, but it wasn't very funny at the time".*

Muriel Cobern was at home with her mother in Kennet Place that morning and has clear memories of the incident. *"I was 12 years old, there was an air raid warning around midday followed by two explosions clearly heard in Marlborough. Returning Home Guard members soon spread the word about what had happened. They were assembled at Red Post, Manton Down, watching the display when one of the pilots dropped a note warning them to scatter as an enemy plane was nearby. Almost immediately it was overhead and dropped two bombs in a field near the Devil's Den. Luckily it missed the cottage, which in those days still stood opposite the ancient monument".*

In 1940 Roger Peck was 14 years old and living at Overton. *"I heard the explosions and ran there with my friends. It [the location] was several miles away. We went up the track beside North Farm and when we arrived found a dead Sparrow, some bomb fragments, which were still warm, and two craters about 20 feet across and 8 to 10 feet deep. The bombs landed on the downs north of the Devil's Den towards Totterdown".*

There was much speculation as to why a lone German bomber should have been flying over Marlborough on a Sunday in broad daylight, as Muriel Cobern recalls. *"The incident caused a wave of spy fever in Marlborough, some people said that the plane was being chased by British fighters and dropped its two remaining bombs at random in order to lighten itself and so gain height and escape, but many saw a more sinister reason and thought that the Germans had prior knowledge of the exercise."* Throughout the summer and early autumn of 1940 - a period now universally referred to as 'The Battle of Britain' - it was not uncommon for German aircraft to be seen in the skies over Wiltshire. However, by the end of October Luftwaffe daylight activity over Britain had largely petered out, but in order to establish the level and accuracy of previous bombing operations lone aircraft would often undertake daylight photo-reconnaissance missions - the previous night there had been 18 separate raids on Bristol, the Midlands, Manchester and Liverpool. The weather on 27th October was overcast and the Luftwaffe would have almost certainly used the cloudy conditions to their advantage, as they attempted to penetrate Britain's defences.

To navigate in daylight pilots would often follow natural or manmade features of the landscape, such as rivers, roads or railway lines, and there's a possibility that the aircraft was following the northerly course of the Midland and South Western Junction Railway. On reaching Marlborough its crew may have noticed the large gathering of people on Manton Down and

**Above:** Three Spitfires from 609 Squadron taking off from Middle Wallop during the summer of 1940.

**Left:** Flying Officer Ostaszewski one of three 609 Squadron pilots vectored to intercept the German bomber that attacked the Home Guard on the morning of 27th October 1940 (Both pictures reproduced by kind permission of 609 (WR) Squadron Association).

**Below:** Upavon airfield pictured during October 2010. It was in this general area that P/O Baillon's Spitfire crashed following its encounter with the German plane.

decided to liven things up a bit. However, as Muriel Corbern has already mentioned, many people believed the German plane was being chased by the Hurricanes that had been scheduled to close the exercise and simply dropped its bombs to make a speedy escape.

George Lanfear was on Manton Down with the Overton Platoon throughout the exercise and was later told that after the German plane had left the area it shot down a Spitfire. Amazingly, a search through records held at the National Archives, Kew has proved that a German bomber did shoot down a Spitfire at precisely the right time and it crashed some 10 miles south of Marlborough near Upavon airfield!

The bomber had been tracked (probably by the pursuing Hurricanes) and its course passed onto the Middle Wallop Operation's Room where the Duty Controller, F/Lt. Fieldsend, vectored three Spitfires from Green Section, B Flight, 609 Squadron, towards it. The Spitfires had taken off from Middle Wallop at 11:25am on a routine patrol and were at 10,000 feet about 10 miles west of the airfield. When they first spotted the German plane it was flying in a south-easterly direction towards them. There seems to have been some confusion as to the type of enemy aircraft, as each of the Spitfire's pilots identified it differently. F/O Forshaw (Green 1, Spitfire X4331) thought it was a Heinkel 111, P/O Baillon (Green 2, Spitfire P9503) described it as a Junkers 88 and F/O Ostaszewski (Green 3, Spitfire X4165) thought it was either a Heinkel 111 or Junkers 88! Each Spitfire attacked the German plane and the following is an extract from P/O Baillon's combat report. *"I followed the leader into a separate quarter attack and opened fire at 300 yards closing to about 70 yards with a 5-6 second burst. Oil spurted over the whole of my windscreen and I broke away to the right. I climbed for a few seconds and as the cockpit became filled with oil and fumes, and my visibility forward was nil, I baled out. The machine landed one mile south of Upavon aerodrome and was completely destroyed. I landed nearby uninjured"*. The two surviving Spitfires returned to Middle Wallop and landed at 12:10pm.

Meanwhile, back on Manton Down, General Sir Francis Gathorne-Hardy gave the order for the battalion to dismiss and each platoon was led to separate points on the downs where transport was waiting to take them home. The Special Police, under the supervision of Inspector Kellier, directed the traffic and despite the unexpected turn of events the large crowd dispersed in a very quick and orderly manner - it may not have occurred to many of those present at the time, but considering what had just happened, they'd all had a very lucky escape!

## Operation 'Moonlight Sonata'

On the evening of Thursday November 14th 1940 Roger Peck was at home with his parents in Overton. *"I remember it was a clear moonlit night and just after 7:00 pm we started to hear German planes flying over. They left a huge white vapour trail that must have been a mile wide and stretched from horizon to horizon - it was most impressive!"* Today the sight of vapour trails streaking across our skies are so commonplace that we take little notice, but in 1940 it was a new aesthetic that fascinated everybody.

Unbeknown to those on the ground the first wave of aircraft were from a specialist pathfinder unit, Kampfgruppe 100 (KGr100), whose Heinkel 111 bombers had been specially modified to carry X-Gerat, a radio navigation system. The Germans were following a beam sent from a transmitter on the French coast near Cherbourg that had a northerly bearing, which lay almost directly over Marlborough. As the planes droned menacingly across the Marlborough Downs their sinister shapes were silhouetted against the moonlit sky, and as wave after wave passed so more and more people living below the flight path came out to watch. Keith Light was a schoolboy living in Overton at the time and recalls, *"We had the blackouts up so mother went outside to look and when she came back she said, 'Some poor blighter's having it tonight!' We went out and you could hear the droning of the planes. It went on all night long - we also heard them when they came back"*.

Soon a terrible red glow appeared on the northern horizon and speculation grew as to its location. The answer was not long in coming, because the following morning, in a break with tradition, the BBC gave out the name of the town that had been bombed. It was a name that will live on forever in British history, for the place in question was the medieval cathedral city of Coventry. The destruction of its city centre was so complete that to hide the truth would have been an impossible and counterproductive task. The British government was also looking for help from the outside world, particularly the United States, and it thought that by publicising the destruction of this once beautiful city world opinion would shift away from Hitler's Germany towards Britain.

## Bending the beams

The German X-Gerat equipment was extremely precise and could achieve bombing accuracy that had previously been thought impossible, even during daylight. For this reason British scientists worked feverishly to develop a system of countermeasures and one idea, commonly referred to as bending the beams, was to send out another beam in a slightly different direction. The deception was reasonably successful and caused many German pilots to become disorientated, forcing them to aimlessly drop their bombs before turning for home.

This may have been what occurred on the evening of Friday 22nd November 1940. John Day and his sister Mary, who both lived at Hill's Farm, Lambourn Woodlands, decided to cycle down into Ramsbury to see a film show in the Memorial Hall. They had got as far as Membury Lodge when they heard the distinctive sound of a German bomber heading in a westerly direction - it was a dark night making it difficult to establish exactly what type of plane it was. Suddenly they heard three explosions and a few moments later the German plane flew over again, but in the opposite direction. The following morning Gordon Starling, who was then a young schoolboy living in Ramsbury, decided to try and find where the bombs had landed and before too long discovered the first crater near Ramsbury's reservoir, which sits on the hill above Crowood House. The other bombs had fallen harmlessly in Love's Copse.

## A hole in the road

On the night of Sunday 16th March 1941, 184 German bombers, a mixture of Junkers 88s and Heinkel 111s, attacked Bristol. One of the bombers got caught in the beams from searchlight units at Mildenhall and Manton Down. Bob Curnick was on Home Guard duty that evening and recalls. *"I presume the German pilot got fed up with these searchlights handing him from one to another and decided to drop some bombs. One landed at an isolated farm near Mildenhall Woodlands and another in the middle of the Marlborough/Rockley road, about 200 yards the Marlborough side of the Old Eagle cottages. Most of the rubble from the crater went out into the field. At the same time a man from Wootton Bassett was driving home in his Austin Ruby car and drove straight into the crater, which was about 10 feet deep. Fortunately the driver was rescued and taken to Savernake Hospital where he made a full recovery"*.

# The mystery of the German bomber

Some years ago, whilst I was researching 'Savernake at War', Vonnie Dickens from Wootton Rivers told me about a German bomber that crashed on farmland to the west of Savernake forest, somewhere between her childhood home at Kingstone Cottages, Cadley and Wootton Rivers. She recalls, *"I was playing with two of my friends from Cadley. We were out in a hayfield and decided to make an air raid shelter from hay. Suddenly, to our horror, this German plane flew over very low. I looked up and could see the black crosses on it. We just stood frozen to the spot and could see in the open door of the plane a German soldier with a rifle. It crashed in a field nearby and for years afterwards we always called the place where it came down the aeroplane field".*

This story intrigued me and I searched through numerous books and records in an attempt to establish the aircraft's identity. Unfortunately I was unable to match the crash with any official record and reluctantly dismissed the story as the product of a young child's over active imagination.

However, more recently other stories have come to light that have made me think again. John Mundy contacted me via email from his home in the United States. His father, Tom, was in the Marlborough Home Guard and was often on duty near Brown's farm on the western edge of the forest, a mile or so north of Cadley. John recalls, *"I remember my father would go out on night patrols. One evening they captured a Luftwaffe pilot that had parachuted from a damaged plane. My father took the pilot into Marlborough in his private car, as the Home Guard had little transport of their own. It was a two door Morris 8 and so my father had another Home Guard sit in the back seat and the pilot beside him in the front. The farm track back to the Salisbury road was very bumpy and the pilot, who spoke good English, asked my father if the guard in the back would put the safety catch on his rifle!"*

David Smith from Marlborough also remembers stories about a German bomber that crashed in the area. *"A German plane crashed between Marlborough and Ramsbury and the Home Guard from both places headed for the crash site. Marlborough got there first and took the plane's machine guns, but the crash location was within Ramsbury's parish boundary and the Ramsbury Platoon thought the weapons should be theirs. This caused some friction between the platoons, but Marlborough still held onto the guns!"*

In 1949 Albert Dean from Pewsey started working for Heard and Leader at their garage in London Road, Marlborough. Three of the mechanics that worked with him at that time were 'Monty' Heard, 'Taffy' Baulch and Charlie Burden. They had all served in the Marlborough Home Guard during the war and often talked about the time they were called out to the site of a crashed German bomber, which came down north of the town somewhere between Rockley and Mildenhall Woodlands.

The previous stories have a few facts to back them up, as the Marlborough College Archive holds a couple of references that may be related to the incident. One comes from a collection of wartime memories from students of The City of London School and states, *"A German plane was shot down near Marlborough and its Spandau machine gun, plus a large quantity of ammunition, was recovered and handed to the 6th Battalion, Wilts LDV (Home Guard). A pamphlet was printed on the handling of the weapon".* Fortunately a copy of this pamphlet has survived and the original is in the City of London School archives. The CLS archivist, Mr Terry Heard, has kindly provided me with a copy. From this it appears that the 'Spandau' was in reality a MG15 7.9mm machine gun, typical of the armament carried by German bombers during the early war period. David Smith has clear memories of two 'Spandau' machine guns being adapted to fit onto a couple of pre-war Carden-Lloyd carriers that belonged to the college.

Harry Sheppard was seven years old in 1940 and living at Hillview Farm, which lies about a mile to the west of Aldbourne along the Marlborough Road. The story that follows may have possible links with Davis Smith's earlier account. *"A German plane flew over during the daytime and it was really smoking. I was up at the farm and saw two chaps parachute out. They were*

Germans and they landed in a meadow on the Marlborough side of the farm, which caused a great deal of excitement. We rushed out into the field to see them and they seemed a bit shaken up. I'm not sure where the plane crashed because I was more interested in these German parachutists - I'd never seen anything like it before in my life. Low and behold, and I don't know how they got there so quickly, but a great heap of Home Guard [from Aldbourne] turned up to capture them. One or two of them were carrying rifles and wearing uniform, but the majority were in civilian clothing and armed with sticks. Mother was there and asked the Germans if they would like a cup of tea, but the man in charge of the Home Guard told her that 'there wasn't time for that'. The Germans went along quietly, which was probably just as well, because we later found out that nobody had any ammunition for the rifles!"

Unfortunately I cannot be certain that any of these stories are related, but hope that by publishing the facts somebody will one day be able to identify the German plane or planes.

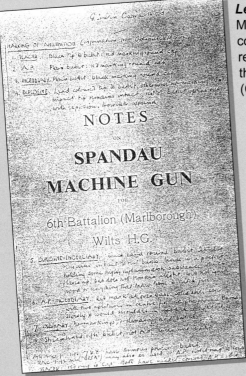

*Left:* The cover of a pamphlet written and produced at Marlborough College, as a guide to the workings of a couple of German MG15 machine guns. The guns were recovered from an enemy aircraft that crashed early in the war and given to the college by the Home Guard. (City of London School)

*Below:* An example of a German MG15 machine gun. When mounted in an aircraft the bipod was removed and different sights fitted. (By kind permission of the Infantry & Small Arms School Corps Weapons Collection, Warminister)

# Spy mania

During the early months of the war the country was gripped by a wave of spy mania, as the government had encouraged people to be vigilant and treat strangers with suspicion. In the months leading up to the outbreak of war thousands of refugees had entered Britain from the Continent and the authorities were fearful that Germany had used this situation to flood the country with Nazi agents or spies. To emphasise this point the Ministry of Information issued many posters warning of the danger, including a series of eight with the slogan 'Careless talk costs lives'. They were designed by Fougasse, which was the pseudonym used by the cartoonist Kenneth Cyril Bird, and they were very successful in getting the message across in an amusing way. The drawings show Hitler, who is sometimes accompanied by Goring, in the most ridiculous locations snooping on unsuspecting members of the public.

The Nazi propaganda machine was anxious to exploit the feeling that spies were everywhere and it's English speaking mouthpiece 'Lord Haw Haw' helped perpetuate the situation through regular radio broadcasts. The nickname 'Lord Haw Haw' was first given to announcers on the English speaking German propaganda radio programme 'Germany Calling' by the Daily Express radio critic Jonah Barrington when he wrote 'He speaks English of the haw-haw, dammit-get-out-of-my-way-variety'. Broadcasts were made regularly throughout the war to audiences in Britain from studios in Hamburg and only ended when the British Army overran the city in April 1945. Poor radio reception made it difficult for listeners to tell the various announcer's voices apart and the British media often used the term 'Lord Haw Haw' to describe all English language German broadcasters, although the name is more usually associated with William Joyce the station's most prominent announcer.

The broadcasts were an attempt to demoralise the British population by spreading rumours to make people believe there were spies on every corner. The announcers also exaggerated British civilian air raid casualties and aircraft and shipping losses. Although it was illegal in Britain to tune into the station it became very popular and had almost as many listeners as the BBC. Each broadcast began with the words 'Germany calling, Germany calling', but because Joyce had broken his nose as a young boy his words sounded like, 'Jarmany calling, Jarmany calling'. During the early months of the war Joyce caused alarm with his tales of a Fifth Column and his accurate descriptions of public clocks that had either stopped or were showing incorrect time. Muriel Cobern remembers that during one of his broadcasts he quite correctly stated that the clock on St Mary's church, at the eastern end of Marlborough's High Street, was 3 minutes slow!

Many rumours circulated Marlborough during 1940, some were false and others just plain stupid, but even the most sceptical could not ignore them all, and Muriel recalls three examples. *"Whenever the siren sounded a light was seen flashing from the college archway over the Bath Road; A man living at Temple Farm used to wander about the downs at night with a revolver, he was arrested as a spy, taken to the Tower and shot; and a man who kept a roadside café at Clench Common was arrested as a spy"*.

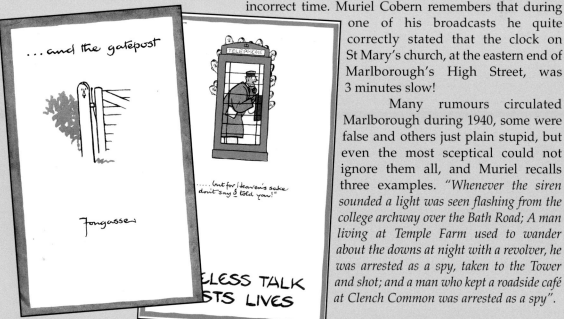

# 4. Uniforms and weapons

## Uniforms

Soon after hearing about the formation of the LDV German radio broadcast a furious announcement in English on the subject, stating *"The preparations which are being made all over England to arm the civilian population for guerrilla warfare are contrary to the rules of international law. German official quarters warn the misled British public and remind them of the fate of the Polish francs-tireurs and gangs of murderers. Civilians who take up arms against German soldiers are, under international law, no better than murderers, whether they are priests or bank clerks. British people, you will do well to heed our warning."* The British government took this threat very seriously and to prevent members of the LDV being shot by the Germans as terrorists decided it was imperative they were provided with some sort of uniform as quickly as possible, no matter how crude it might be.

Early volunteers reported for duty wearing their everyday civilian clothing, but in order to comply with international law were soon issued with a simple khaki armband marked LDV, which was usually worn on the right sleeve. Those with previous military service, especially officers, often wore their old uniforms and assumed their old rank, although the use of rank was officially frowned upon.

Within a week of the LDV's formation 90,000 denim overalls had been made available nationally, as well as 250,000 field service caps. The denims were similar in design to the British army battledress but were intended as soldiers working clothing to be worn over uniforms to keep them free from dirt and grease. For this reason the denims were always one size larger than the battledress equivalent, which made it difficult for newly attired members of the LDV to appear smartly dressed. This was compounded by the fact that the regular army had first claim on overalls, so those that remained were often far too large or small.

During August 1940 it was announced that the name of the new force was to change from Local Defence Volunteers to Home Guard. Because of wartime shortages a patch, printed with the words 'Home Guard', was given out, which was to be sewn on to the old armbands covering the letters LDV.

The issue of denims was designed as a stopgap measure. They were made from thin cotton material making them totally unsuitable for winter wear. Unfortunately, during 1940, only a few of the warmer 1937 pattern woollen army battledresses had been made available for Home Guard use and it was May 1941 before the battalion was fully kitted out with these uniforms. Therefore, to keep volunteers warm during the winter of 1940/41 a number of greatcoats were issued to the battalion. Unfortunately there were insufficient numbers to go round and at the end of each duty period they had to be handed back into store.

However, by mid 1941 nearly every man in the battalion had received a woollen battledress, greatcoat, service respirator, boots, leather belt, anklets and steel helmet. Ron Bridges remembers the night the Winterbourne Bassett Platoon received their steel helmets. *"Doctor Bradley was the vicar of Winterbourne Bassett - he was a doctor of music. I remember the night we were issued our tin hats. There were four of us on duty in an old empty thatched farm workers cottage.*

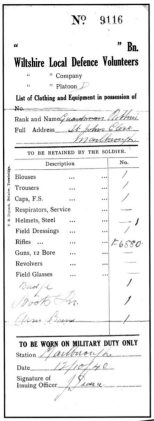

**Far left:** On 12th October 1940 Ronald Robins from Marlborough was issued with a number of items of clothing and equipment and given this check list. Sometime during the following month the list was replaced by a new modified version. More items of clothing and equipment had been added and the 'Wiltshire Local Defence Volunteers' heading replaced by 'Wiltshire Home Guard'. By this time Ronald Robins had been given even more equipment and on 20th November was asked to sign for the new items, as well as the kit already in his possession, and given one of the new checklists to keep as a record (near left).

**Below:** On joining the force all volunteers had to complete and sign form AF W3066. By late 1940 the original LDV enrolment form (left) had been replaced by a slightly modified Home Guard version (right).

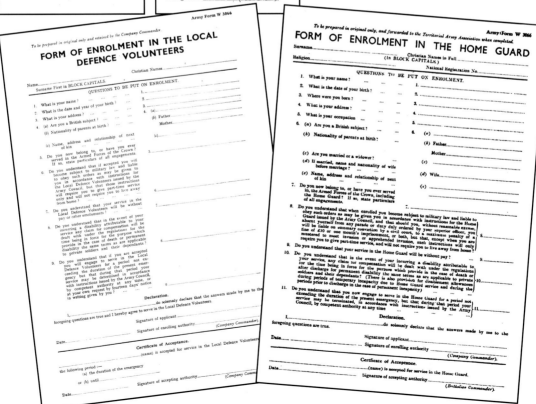

*It had a large fireplace and we kept a fire lit while we were on duty. We were sitting around the fire when Dr Bradley, who was very well spoken said, 'Let's see how it fits?' So he put it on and said 'Yes it fits OK'. John Horton said that we had better give it a test and picked up a poker from beside the fire and whacked him over the head. 'Wow' he said 'I felt that!' and went down as if he'd been knocked out".* Everybody was very alarmed to begin with but quickly realised the vicar was just fooling around.

It was at about this time (mid 1941) that the Home Guard armband was replaced by shoulder titles similar in design to those worn by regular soldiers. During the latter half of the year printed county and battalion shoulder insignia also started to appear on the upper sleeves of uniforms. However, despite this practice being commonplace throughout most of Britain the author has been unable to find any evidence of county and battalion insignia being worn by any members of the Marlborough Battalion.

When the time came for young Home Guards to join the army they were told to report wearing their Home Guard uniforms, as John Bower recalls. *"My father went to see Sgt. Kerr, who was the battalion's quarter-master sergeant, and told him I was going in the army in a months time. Sgt. Kerr said he'd better get me a decent uniform and* [deliberately] *got me one that was too big. When I got into the army I had it tailor made and I got 'two sticks' at Bovington for that!"* Audrey Peck remembers that her brother had to take his Home Guard boots with him when he joined the services. *"He was very cross at the time because his boots were a bit small and he had a hell of a job getting the army to exchange them for a larger size".*

## Weapons
### Shotguns
Because the Marlborough district was, and still is, a predominately rural area a large number of the battalion's volunteers earned their living from the land and many owned shotguns for shooting vermin or game. Most guns were designed to fire either 12 or 16 bore cartridges and

they quickly became the LDV's first real weapon of quantity. To increase numbers a War Office appeal was broadcast on 15th June 1940 asking members of the public to loan shotguns to the new force for the duration of hostilities.

Conventional shot could only kill at short range so special cartridges containing a single solid ball and marked with the War Department broad arrow were issued to the LDV. According to LDV Instruction Sheet No. 5, dated July 1940, the cartridges were accurate up to 100 yards and the gun was to be handled in exactly the same way as against game, with the usual forward allowance for moving bodies. At these distances the solid ball was capable of causing awful injuries and probably contravened Geneva Convention rules, but desperate times demanded desperate measures!

### Rifles
As previously mentioned, in June 1940 small quantities of .303 Short Magazine Lee Enfield (SMLE) Rifles were issued to the LDV and more followed including a number of P14s, which like the SMLE fired .303 ammunition. Towards the end of the year a quantity of Ross rifles of First World War vintage arrived from Canada. These weapons fired a different type of cartridge to the

SMLE and were unpopular, as the smallest amount of dirt easily damaged the mechanism. On 5th November William Young received instructions stating that the Avebury Platoon was to exchange its SMLEs and P14s for Ross rifles. Young was not best pleased because before handing them back all the weapons had to be collected from the men, checked and signed for, which created a lot of extra work.

The Ramsbury Platoon also received a number of Ross rifles, as 'Tiny' Watts recalls. *"The Ross was a long barrelled rifle, very accurate but not so good for field work, as the breach worked on a quick thread that was very prone to jam with the smallest amount of dirt. On the Sunday we were issued with the Ross rifles we carried out some small skirmish movements in the water meadows. Whilst lying in a dry ditch I removed the bolt from the rifle, only to find I couldn't replace it (kid with a new toy!). We moved on so I put the bolt in my pocket. When we paraded for dismissal and the arms were inspected nobody noticed [that the bolt was missing]. By the next parade I'd mastered it!"*

The Ross was so unpopular that some platoons, including Avebury, were reissued with SMLEs, but this was just a stopgap measure and by the middle of 1941 they had all been withdrawn and replaced by US P17 rifles, which like the Canadian Ross, had been manufactured during the First World War. The British government purchased 615,000 of these weapons during 1940 plus a large quantity of ammunition. Unfortunately the P17s were a different calibre to the Lee Enfield (.300 as opposed to .303) and to prevent mishaps the P17s had red bands painted round their barrels.

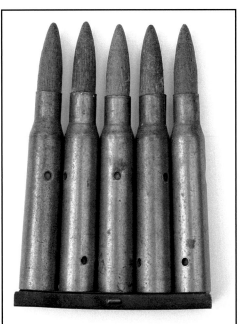

***Above:*** For drill purposes units of the Home Guard issued with US P17 rifles often used dummy rounds instead of live ammunition. America supplied Britain with empty 30.60 cartridge cases, which then had wooden bullet shaped plugs inserted. Most of the cartridges were made by the Frankford Arsenal of Philadelphia and were head stamped FA followed by the date of manufacture.

The American rifles started to appear in the Marlborough area during July 1941 and William Young recorded their arrival at Avebury in his diary entry for Tuesday 8th August. *"Major Giffard informed me that all our Short Lee Enfield rifles have to be handed in sometime this week and we are to be issued with the new US .300 rifles instead. I have therefore arranged for my platoon to hand in their rifles to me on Thursday evening so that Major Giffard can change them, along with the .303 ammunition, on Friday. I hope this will be the last time we shall have to change our rifles!"* Unfortunately six men from Young's platoon failed to hand in their weapons on time and the following day he had to personally visit each man's home and retrieve them.

At the end of the First World War, when the P17 and Ross rifles were taken out of service by their respective governments, they were covered in grease, crated and placed in storage. By 1940 the grease had solidified and had to be removed from the weapons before they could be used. *"We were eventually issued with Canadian Ross rifles"*, recalls Eddy Witts. *"They were covered in grease and it took me a fortnight to clean mine up by gradually rubbing away at it."*

Dickie Brown from Durley remembers being issued with a rifle, but no ammunition. *"After Dunkirk lots of troops were sent to Tottenham House. One night while I was on duty one of the soldiers said to me 'Have you got any ammunition for that rifle?' I said 'no'. 'Oh', he said, 'fat lot of good that will be'. Next night when he came down to see me his pockets were bulging with ammunition! I'm not sure if it was a good or bad thing. You must remember that half the people in the LDV had never handled a rifle or shotgun in their lives - I was lucky, as I'd been brought up with guns. We had a Col. Snow who used to come round periodically during the night to see if all was well. He used to pull up in his car wind the window down and say 'Is everything alright?' Whoever was on duty would go out, rifle under arm, put one foot on the car's running board and talk to the Colonel through the open window. When he said 'Well, good get on with it' they put their foot down, but at the same time accidentally pull the rifle's trigger. The near side door of Col. Snow's car ended up with about half-a-dozen holes in it!"*

One wonders how Col. Snow tolerated this persistent damage to his vehicle because he did not appear to have been blessed with a great sense of humour, as the following incident, recalled by George Cady, demonstrates. *"Col. Snow was what I called a real old fashioned Indian Colonel - full of it! Most mornings he used to catch the London train at Savernake station and one day shouted to the porter 'How long is the train going to be?' to which he received the reply, 'About two coaches and an engine'. The colonel was not very amused and told the porter that when he got to Paddington station he would report him for insubordination!"*

## Revolvers

All Home Guard officers were issued with a service revolver, webbing belt and holster - the most common type of pistol was the .38 Webley. Occasionally lower ranks were also issued with a sidearm, as recalled by Bill Eastmond a Private in the East Grafton Platoon. *"Because I had a motor cycle they made me a dispatch rider and I was given an extra petrol ration. I couldn't carry a rifle* [when riding the bike] *so was issued with a revolver and just five rounds of ammunition. I said 'what do I do when I run out, throw the gun at them?'"*

## Machine Carbines

During the spring of 1941 the battalion received a number of American Thompson sub-machine guns and one was given to the Ramsbury Platoon, as 'Tiny' Watts recalls. *"The platoon was issued with one Thompson sub-machine gun, which was held by Sgt. Smith. I remember it had a drum magazine like American gangsters!"* These weapons had earned themselves a fearsome reputation following their portrayal in numerous 1930's US gangster movies, where they were commonly referred to as 'Tommy guns' or 'Chicago pianos'. The gun fired a .45 calibre round at a rate of about 650 rounds per minute, which made it very effective at stopping an attacker and extremely popular with the men. Unfortunately it was very heavy, weighing in at 15lbs, and expensive, as it was built to a very high standard - each gun cost the British government $225 (about £55). Its effectiveness also made it popular with other units of the British army, such as the commandos, and by March 1942 all 'Tommy guns' had been withdrawn from Home Guard service.

The Sten gun replaced the 'Tommy gun' and nearly 3,000 of these weapons were eventually issued to the Wiltshire Home Guard. It was a strange, ugly looking gun but it had a rapid rate of fire and weighing just 8lbs fully loaded was much lighter than the Thompson. It was also much cheaper to manufacture, as many of its component parts were made from mild steel pressings. Each weapon purportedly cost two pounds seven shillings (£2.35) and the Press gave it several disparaging nicknames including 'the drain pipe gun' and 'the Woolworth gun'! The name Sten was derived from the first letters of the designer's surnames ('S' for Shepherd, 'T' for Turpin) plus its country of origin ('EN' for England).

All units of the Marlborough Battalion eventually received Stens and the Baydon platoon was no exception, as Len Richardson recalls, *"I used the old Sten gun. They were very handy because you could shoot them from the hip, but if you weren't careful you could pinch your fingers"*. This was a common complaint, as the ejection hole for spent cartridges was on the side of the barrel just where the fingers of the left hand gripped the gun. A simple guard was fitted to the Sten MkIII but earlier models were unprotected, and it was easy for a finger to be caught by the moving breechblock. Bill Eastmond remembers that the East Grafton Platoon had two Stens. *"When I used the gun it always seemed to fire into the ground!"*

**Below:** A MKIII 9mm machine carbine, better known as the Sten gun, surrounded by a small selection of the numerous official and unofficial manuals produced during the war. The majority of the privately published booklets were aimed at the Home Guard and were bought in their thousands, mainly by officers and NCOs of the force, whose duty was to teach members of their unit how to handle and fire the weapon.

Note the gun's simple finger guard just in front of the ejection hole for spent cartridge cases, which was fitted to the MKIII to prevent fingers of the left hand being caught by the moving breechblock.

MANUAL OF THE STEN GUN

By Lieut. E. W. MANDERS and W. BENTLY CAPPER

MARK I — Components — Stripping

MARK II — Assembling — Loading

MARK III — 1/6

WITH NOTES ON THE NORTHOVER

MANUAL OF MODERN AUTOMATIC GUNS

STEN, BREN, LEWIS THOMPSON, VICKERS BROWNING ETC., ETC.

LOADING, FIRING DETAILS of MECHANISM STOPPAGES AND IMMEDIATE ACTION STRIPPING & ASSEMBLING ETC. ETC.

SPECIALLY PREPARED FOR HOME GUARD & SERVICE USE

1/- 1/-

BERNARDS, PUBLISHERS, LTD. 73 THE GRAMPIANS, WESTERN GATE, LONDON, W.6

NOT TO BE PUBLISHED
The information given in this document is not to be communicated, either directly or indirectly, to the Press or to any person not holding an official position in His Majesty's Service.

*Notified in A.C.Is. 22nd August, 1942*

26
G.S. Publications
780

**Small Arms Training**

Volume I, Pamphlet No. 22

Sten Machine Carbine

1942

*Crown Copyright Reserved*

*By Command of the Army Council,*

THE WAR OFFICE, 22nd August, 1942

Printed under the Authority of HIS MAJESTY'S STATIONERY OFFICE by Keliher, Hudson & Kearns, Ltd., London, S.E.1.

KNOW YOUR WEAPONS : Nº 5

STEN AND

Flash Eliminator
Foresight
Sling Swivel
Magazine Housing
Magazine Catch
Magazine
Ejection Opening
Breech Block
Cocking Handle
Return Spring
Backsight
Wooden Hand Grip
Change Lever
Trigger Pin
Trigger Guard
Return Spring Housing
Tubular Butt

BREN GUNS

1/- net.

NICHOLSON N&W & WATSON

George Johnson from Marlborough had to use a Sten during a proficiency test in woodland near Ogbourne St George, which involved firing at targets placed up in trees, and in order to fully appreciate the Sten's many vices the Ramsbury Platoon had the novel idea of shooting at tin cans floating down the River Kennet.

## Machine Guns

The Lewis gun was the light machine gun most commonly used by the 6th Battalion. It was originally designed with an aluminium barrel-casing which used the muzzle blast to draw air into the gun for cooling purposes. There was some doubt as to whether the cooling tube actually worked and many of the Home Guard's Lewis guns were old air cooled weapons that had been fitted to aircraft during the First World War. However, prolonged bursts of fire could overheat and distort the barrel and the 1940 manual '.300 Lewis Machine Gun for the Home Guard' published in Wiltshire by The Bravon Ledger Co warned '…fire should be delivered in short bursts of approximately 5 rounds each. The normal rate of fire is five bursts a minute'.

The Ogbourne St Andrew Platoon was issued with a Lewis Gun and Bob Curnick recalls its arrival. *"One day an officer addressed us wanting to know if any of us had attended a Public School and had OCTU army training. Since there was no response to his question he then enquired if any of us had been to Grammar School. Frank and I replied in the affirmative. This revelation meant that we received instruction on the care and use of a machine gun. This was a World War 1 Lewis machine gun, which was rather heavy and needed two men to carry it"*. Because other venues suitable for instructing, such as the village hut and school, were busy on Sunday mornings it was decided that Bob and his brother Frank should receive their training over the following seven weeks in the Wheatsheaf public house, starting at 10am. *"After milking, washing up, sterilising, feeding livestock and having our breakfast it was difficult to get there by 10am. Saturday night was by far the busiest night of the week for the local pub. After serving beer and cigarettes right up to 10:30pm the landlord and his wife were far too tired to do any cleaning up. I cannot begin to describe how revolting the saloon bar was at 10am on a Sunday morning. The floor, tables and chairs awash with stale beer and cigarette stubs, no door or windows open, curtains and blackout curtains still in place and reeking of stale tobacco smoke. We had to lie down on the floor and were instructed on how to cope with the machine gun when it jammed. I can fully recommend two hours work in a stale saloon bar to put one off smoking and excessive drinking for life!"*

After several months of looking after the Lewis gun Bob and his brother were getting rather tired of carrying it around on parades and exercises. Then one Sunday morning while the officer in charge was inspecting weapons Bob had a bright idea. *"When he saw the dust on the machine gun he told us that if we didn't keep the gun cleaner it would be taken from us. The light dawned - I made sure we didn't clean it before the next inspection and were promptly relieved of it. By then smaller Sten machine guns had arrived, which were much lighter to carry!"*

## Hand Grenades

Immediately following the formation of the LDV the School of Military Engineering, Chatham, hastily put together a pamphlet entitled 'The Home Made Molotov Cocktail'. It was produced to give as many people as possible all the information they needed to quickly manufacture cheap, simple firebombs for use against enemy tanks and vehicles. On the opening page the pamphlet states; *'The general idea is that a number of these bombs shall be thrown by several attackers at close range at a halted or slow moving vehicle…These bombs consist generally of a very inflammable petrol and oil mixture contained in a common glass bottle which breaks on contact with the target. The bottle carries with it a flaming fuse which starts the fire'.*

Molotov cocktails first appeared during the Spanish civil war and were later used by the Finnish Army to great effect against Red Army tanks during the Russo-Finnish War. The Finns named their firebombs after the Soviet Foreign Minister Vyacheslav Mikhailovich Molotov, as a way of mocking him.

**Above:** The first 'uniforms' given to members of the force were cloth armbands printed with the letters LDV

**Left:** During the early months of the Home Guard's existence improvisation was the key when providing the force with anti-tank weapons. Thousands of petrol bombs, known as Molotov cocktails, were made using old glass bottles with rag wicks.

**Right:** By August 1940 the name of the force had changed to Home Guard and patches bearing this title were stitched to the right arms of its newly issued denim uniforms.

**Left:** By 1941 most members of the Home Guard had been issued with 1937 pattern battledress uniforms plus an assortment of other equipment. In this picture Jack Light from Overton is wearing a service respirator, leather belt, ammunition pouches, side cap, leather gaiters, ammunition boots and carries a P17 rifle. (Keith Light)

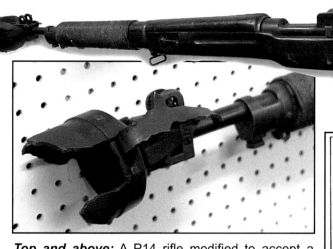

**Top and above:** A P14 rifle modified to accept a grenade cup discharger. Note the string wound around the barrel and stock to give added strength. The cup on this example has been damaged as a result of the premature detonation of a grenade. (By kind permission of the Infantry & Small Arms School Corps Weapons Collection, Warminister)

**Right:** Looking more like a large toffee apple than a grenade the 'Sticky Bomb' was designed as an anti-tank weapon. It entered service with the Home Guard during 1941 and its sticky nature made it very dangerous to the user, as this period cartoon illustrates. (Home Guard Humour, Amberley Publishing, 2010)

**Below left and right:** While in storage the bomb's sticky ball was protected by two metal hemispheres. However, to prevent accidents during exercises a white painted wooden dummy grenade, which had a metal ring around its middle to add weight, was often used. (By kind permission of the Infantry & Small Arms School Corps Weapons Collection, Warminister).

THE STICKY BOMB

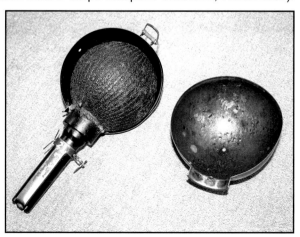

The Molotov Cocktail was a very crude and unpredictable weapon, but was popular with Home Guard platoons as hundreds could be made quickly and cheaply using old bottles, rags and petrol. It was replaced a little later in the war by the factory produced No.76 Self-Igniting Phosphorous (SIP) Grenade.

The No.36M Mills Bomb eventually became the Home Guard's principle hand grenade. It had a very distinctive 'pineapple' shape and had been widely used by the British Army during the First World War. There were several sites in the Marlborough battalion area that were regularly used for grenade practice, such as the disused Dodsdown sandpits near Wilton, the valley near the sewage works just east of Lockeridge House and Rough Down rifle range north of Marlborough common.

Working with live grenades could be a very dangerous business, as the following incidents clearly illustrate. On 7th December 1941 during live grenade practice at the Rough Down rifle range Sergeant George Edward Smith, a permanent Home Guard instructor attached to the Marlborough battalion, had to act very quickly to prevent a very serious accident. About 25 men from 'C' Company were under instruction when one of the men, whilst in the act of throwing a grenade, struck one of the sandbags around the edge of the throwing pit. The bomb landed on top of the bags and then rolled down amongst other live bombs and detonators. Sergeant Smith immediately ordered all men to lie down and then ran forward, picked up the bomb, and just managed to throw it clear before it exploded. As a result of this gallant act Sergeant Smith was awarded the British Empire Medal (BEM).

Just over six months later, on the morning of 24th May 1942, another BEM was won by Sergeant Frederick John Leslie Rosier who had recently returned from a bombing course and was instructing the Wilton Platoon in grenade throwing at the Dodsdown sandpits. According to Bill Eastmond, Ronnie Cox from Wexcombe had just removed the pin from a grenade and was about to throw it when it slipped from his grasp. It rolled under a board beside a box of live grenades and Sergeant Rosier quickly ordered all the men to take cover before extracting the bomb and throwing it out of the pit - the grenade exploded as soon as it hit the ground.

A man of average build was capable of throwing a grenade about 30 yards, but by fitting a grenade cup discharger to the barrel of a rifle the range could be increased by as much as four or five times. The P14, P17 and SMLE were all capable of accepting a cup discharger and modified weapons were known as EY rifles - the EY standing for Ernest Youlle its inventor. The Wiltshire Home Guard had about 790 of these weapons in its arsenal, which roughly equated to about 60 per battalion. The blank round used to throw a Mills Bomb contained more propellant than a normal .303 round and sometimes rifle barrels would distort or even burst under the extra pressure! To help prevent this happening string or copper wire was wound around the barrel to give it added strength. Bill Eastmond remembers using an EY Rifle, which he called a cup discharger, in a field just outside Wilton beside the Wexcombe road. *"We used to fire the cup discharger using dummy grenades at a piece of propped up corrugated tin. You put the butt of the rifle into the ground so that it didn't jump and aimed using guess work"*. George Johnson also remembers using a cup discharger. *"We used to do our practice at the college meadows near the cricket pitch and would get down behind the banks in case one misfired. You would pull the pin out of the grenade, drop it into the cup and then fire the rifle. The grenade would usually go 50 yards or so"*.

Another type of grenade Bill Eastmond recalls using was the 'Sticky Bomb' or, as it was officially known, the No.74 Grenade. The bomb was quickly developed during the early months of the Second World War as a stopgap anti-tank weapon. It consisted of a short handle, which was screwed into a round hollow glass ball that contained 20 ounces of pure nitro-glycerine. The glass ball was covered with a tight fitting sock that was coated with a very sticky adhesive. To prevent the adhesive surface accidentally sticking to other objects two metal hemispheres were clamped around it.

**Above:** Many Home Guard veterans have described the Northover Projector as looking like a drainpipe on legs and this contemporary drawing reinforces that image. The projector was designed to fire a number of grenades including the No. 76 SIP (also known as the AW Bomb) and for safety reasons they were stored twenty-four at a time in crates like the example shown below. Beside the crate are two rubber practice rounds which have the words 'Drill Projectile' moulded on the base (See inset below).

**Left:** Screwed inside the crate's lid was an enamel plate entitled 'Precautions' that gave warnings and advice on the best way to handle and store the bombs.

# PRECAUTIONS

**A W BOMBS** fire instantly on breaking in air.

If fire is started accidentally, use water freely.

Store bombs (preferably in cases) in cool place, under water if possible.

Do not store near inflammable material.

Avoid storing many bombs close together if possible.

Stringent precautions must be taken to avoid cracking bombs during handling.

The caps must never be removed.

**Main picture:** This beautiful model of a Spigot Mortar belongs to Andrew Tilley from Hungerford. It was made by his grandfather, who served in the Hungerford Home Guard, and was used as a prop to demonstrate the weapon's main features to members of his section.

**Left:** An original dummy Spigot mortar projectile. (By kind permission of the Infantry & Small Arms School Corps Weapons Collection, Warminister).

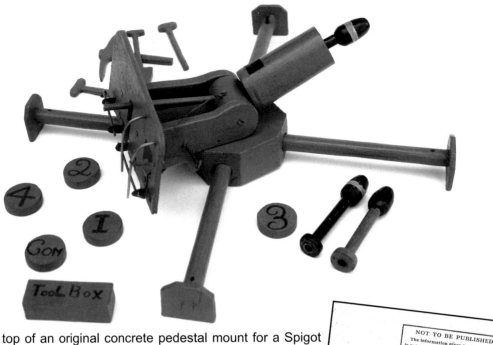

**Below:** The top of an original concrete pedestal mount for a Spigot Mortar. The pedestal was about 4ft high and normally surrounded by a weapon pit. When in position the mortar rotated about the stainless steel pin protruding from the top. This example was pictured outside the Vickers factory at South Marston near Swindon in 1990.

**Right:** An original Spigot Mortar training manual issued to Marlborough's 'A' Company.

NOT TO BE PUBLISHED
The information given in this document is not to be communicated, either directly or indirectly, to the Press or to any person not holding an official position in His Majesty's Service.

26
G.S. Publications
790

Notified in
A.C.Is.
7th November,
1942

# Small Arms Training
Volume I, Pamphlet No. 23

## The 29-mm. Spigot Mortar

### 1942

(This ... sedes the 29-mm. Spigot Mortar ... Instruction (Provisional, 1941))

Crown ... right Reserved

By ... mand of the Army Council,

... WAR OFFICE,

Printed ... by Reither, Hudson & Kearns, Ltd., London, S.E.1.

To use the bomb the two hemispheres were removed by pulling out a safety pin, then, to arm the weapon a second pin was withdrawn from the handle. A firing lever was held in place until the bomb was successfully stuck to its target, but once released the grenade would detonate in just five seconds. Bill and other members of the East Grafton Platoon practiced with their 'sticky bombs' in the Dodsdown sandpits. *"We used to stick the bombs to the old metal skips that had been used to move clay for brick making. You had to walk away from the target at an angle so that the handle of the bomb did not hit you when it exploded!"*

## Northover Projector

The Northover Projector was a strange looking weapon that had been designed by a Major Northover who was an officer in the Home Guard - it entered service during the summer of 1941.

The weapon's purpose was to project grenades and it was capable of firing No.36, No.68 and No.76 grenades for a distance of about 200 yards. The No.76 SIP is the grenade most commonly associated with the Northover and, as previously mentioned, was the official version of a Molotov cocktail. It was also known as the AW Bomb after its manufacturer Albright and Wilson and was a glass bottle with a highly inflammable filling of phosphorous and naphtha or benzine. In addition a two-inch strip of crude rubber was also added to make the substance sticky so that it would adhere to its target. The bombs had to be handled with great care and came in wooden boxes capable of holding 24 of the grenades. The boxes, which were similar in design to those used for storing beer bottles, had an enamel instruction plate entitled PRECAUTIONS screwed inside the lid and branded on top of the lid were the words: A.W. BOMBS - FRAGILE GLASS - HIGHLY INFLAMMABLE.

*"I remember seeing a Northover Projector fired on Marlborough Common using dummy rounds"*, recalls Peter Piper. *"It was a weird thing that looked like a drainpipe with a couple of wheels attached"*. The Avebury Platoon carried out its first practice with the weapon on Sunday 19th October 1941 firing both dummy and live AW Bombs. For safety reasons the practice took place well away from the village on Avebury Down. Unfortunately some of the platoon's members were away working at Yatesbury Camp, so attendance was poor, but at least this gave everyone present an opportunity to fire the projector twice! The popularity of the Northover soon declined and it was replaced by the Spigot Mortar.

## Spigot Mortar

By October 1942 the Wiltshire Home Guard had received 328 Spigot Mortars and nearly every platoon was given one. It had been invented by a Lieutenant-Colonel Blacker and for this reason was also known as the Blacker Bombard. Just like the Northover Projector it was another strange looking device, but unlike the Northover it could lob a 20lb anti-tank projectile some 200 yards, which made it far more potent.

The weapon needed a crew of five and it sat on a base plate that was attached to four splayed out legs. For static defence the base plate and legs were dispensed with and the mortar was placed over a stainless steel pivot that protruded from the top of a fixed concrete pedestal. During the war Ron Liddiard was a schoolboy living in Chilton Foliat and remembers seeing a firing demonstration at the village recreation ground. *"The weapon was loaded with a dummy projectile and fired diagonally across the field. Everything seemed to happen in slow-motion and the bomb could be clearly seen as it flew through the air from one corner of the field to the other!"*

## Barrel Flame Traps

These traps consisted of 40-gallon steel barrels filled with an inflammable mixture of petrol and gas oil that could be deployed in three different ways:

> 1. A barrel buried or partially buried in a roadside bank was known as a flame fougasse and when ignited could project a stream of burning fuel in a fixed direction - this was the preferred method of use.

2. If there was insufficient time to prepare a flame fougasse then either a demigasse or a hedgehopper could be employed. The demigasse was a barrel lying on its side in the open and was ignited in the same way as a flame fougasse, but was far less accurate, as the barrel was not held solidly in place.

3. The hedgehopper, as its name implies, was designed to hop over hedges. A charge was placed under the barrel slightly off centre and when ignited the barrel would jump about 10 feet vertically and 20 feet horizontally. With luck it would hop over the hedge or fence that was hiding it and land on the other side flooding the area with burning fuel. Accurate timing was essential in order to hit a moving target!

The intention was to site flame traps in places where enemy tanks would have to slow down or even stop, such as roadblocks, narrow bridges or sharp bends. It was an added advantage if the sites were in sunken lanes or cuttings, as this would prevent tanks going off-road. The man in charge of firing the trap had to put himself in a position where he could see the trap's line of fire and the enemy's anticipated direction of approach. After burying a flame fougasse it was vitally important that left over soil was carefully disposed of and tracks concealed preventing observation from the air.

Unfortunately the author has been unable to establish if any live barrel flame traps were actually sited in the Marlborough area. However, official documentation has revealed that the following locations were definitely earmarked for this purpose.

| Grid Ref: | Location |
|---|---|
| 666838 | Burbage Wharf |
| 677836 | Savernake |
| 723847 | Great Bedwyn |
| 732861 | Little Bedwyn |
| 747880 | Froxfield |
| 639898 | Marlborough - Mildenhall Road |
| 635886 | Marlborough - Salisbury Road |
| --------- | Marlborough - London Road |
| 6288 | Marlborough - Granham Hill |
| 6289 | Marlborough - Hyde Lane |
| 5588 | West Kennett |
| 7095 | Aldbourne |
| 6494 | Ogbourne St. George |

On the morning of Sunday September 21st 1941 several members of the Marlborough Battalion, including William Young, George Stevens, Major Giffard, Captain Dyball and Lieutenant Godfrey attended a tank fighting demonstration on a hill north of Bishops Cannings. Some 300 members of the Wiltshire Home Guard from all across the county were present and according to William Young it was a spectacular affair that included the use of flamethrowers, fougasse and hedgehoppers plus firing grenades from Northover Projectors.

As this is such a little known and poorly researched subject the author would be keen to hear from any reader who may have information regarding the deployment and use of barrel flame traps in the Marlborough area.

## The Smith Gun

During 1942 the Wiltshire Home Guard received 110 Smith Guns, which were distributed throughout the county. Just like the Northover Projector and Spigot Mortar it was another strange looking device.

The weapon was designed in 1940 as a stopgap measure to quickly and cheaply replace equipment lost following the Dunkirk evacuation. By 1942 Smith Guns had been issued to the RAF for airfield defence and large numbers were also made available to home based regular army units and the Home Guard. It was a smooth bore, breech-loading weapon that could be pulled along by a car or lorry on its two 48-inch diameter wheels. To fire the gun it first had to be turned over onto its right hand concave wheel, which allowed the gun to rotate about its axle - the left hand wheel offered the gun's crew a limited amount of protection from above. It came with a limber that was also fitted with a pair of 48-inch diameter wheels and could be attached to the gun for towing purposes. On 13th October 1942 members of the Home Guard from all across Wiltshire were invited to attend a demonstration at Larkhill where several guns were in action.

Towards the end of the war the Savernake platoon became a mobile unit and was given a Smith Gun, as Ray Beasley recalls. *The gun was drawn behind a civilian car, but if you travelled too fast its solid rubber tyres would come off!* Ray also remembers that it was important to site the gun on level ground or there was a danger it would jump in the air and the top wheel hit the heads of its crew.

**Right:** An illustration taken from a Home Guard instruction manual showing a Smith Gun being pulled off its wheels into its firing position.

**Below:** A surviving Smith Gun and limber on display at the Royal Armouries Museum, Fort Nelson, Portsmouth.

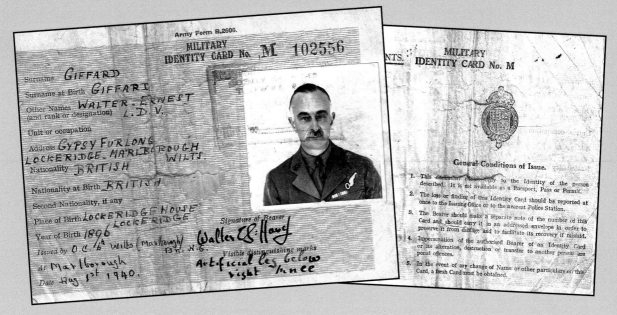

# Home Guard identity documents

**Officers**

At the beginning of July 1940 all army officers were issued with a military identity card (AF B2606) and from 13th July the War Office authorised the issued of the same card to LDV officers. Each officer had to supply a photograph of himself 'in uniform without hat' at his own expense and these cards were carried by the bearer until the Home Guard's stand down in 1944.

The cards came in pads with a counterfoil. They were printed on very thin paper that was coloured pink on the inside where the bearer's personal details were recorded together with his signature and photograph. Once detached from the counterfoil the card was folded in half and presented to the bearer.

The card shown above was issued to Walter Giffard who lived at Gypsy Furlong, Lockeridge. Under the section entitled visible distinguishing marks is written 'Artificial leg below right knee'. When Walter Giffard was 16 years old he tripped whilst out shooting in West Woods, accidentally discharging his shotgun into his right leg, which had to be amputated below the knee. In 1917, despite his disability, he joined the Royal Flying Corps as an observer in balloons and was eventually promoted to the rank of Captain. His identity card photograph shows him wearing his old RFC uniform complete with observer's brevet.

Following the outbreak of WWII Walter Giffard, like many of his generation, was anxious to help in any way he could and was one of the first to join the Marlborough LDV. Initially he was given command of 'B' Company but in March 1943, following Lt. Col. Fuller's departure, he assumed command of the entire Marlborough Battalion.

**Other Ranks**

On 25th June 1940 Marlborough's LDV Platoon Commanders were instructed to sign all their volunteer's National Registration Cards and mark them with an LDV stamp. However, from December 1940 a metal stamp was used to emboss the words 'Battalion' and 'Home Guard' with a gap between the two words where the battalion's details were entered by hand. Unfortunately, because a new-style card was issued during March 1943 very few of the original cards have survived and it's difficult to determine whether the metal stamp was ever used in the Marlborough area.

# 5. Civilian occupations

During the First World War too many skilled workers were allowed to enlist in the armed forces and this created a serious shortage of labour in certain key industries on the Home Front. To prevent this happening again, in 1938 a Schedule of Reserved Occupations was drawn up that excluded many key workers from conscription.

Because Wiltshire was predominately a rural county many of those who volunteered to join the Marlborough Battalion were employed on the land, and as farming was one of the principle reserved occupations a very large percentage of the Battalion's compliment were farm workers. They were joined by other key workers from a long list that included; railway employees; teachers and university lecturers; doctors; police officers; civil servants; students (only for the duration of their studies); utility workers (water, gas, electricity); priests, monks, nuns and anyone in holy orders; journalists and some other media workers; artists involved in propaganda work; anyone running a small business; local authority employees; bank employees and employees of insurance companies; company directors and veterinary surgeons.

Mr H G Edwards worked at Knighton Farm near Ramsbury and recalls, "As head tractor driver

---

IMPORTANT. THIS APPLICATION SHOULD REACH A LOCAL OFFICE OF THE MINISTRY OF LABOUR AND NATIONAL SERVICE NOT LATER THAN 2 DAYS AFTER THE DATE ON WHICH YOU ARE MEDICALLY EXAMINED OR, IN THE CASE OF AN APPLICATION FOR RENEWAL, NOT LATER THAN 14 DAYS BEFORE THE EXPIRATION OF THE PREVIOUS CERTIFICATE.

REGN. No. *WSLD. 35 - 3*

DATE OF REGN.

## NATIONAL SERVICE (ARMED FORCES) ACT, 1939

### APPLICATION BY PERSON LIABLE TO BE CALLED UP FOR MILITARY SERVICE FOR A POSTPONEMENT CERTIFICATE.

(*Note.*—Any person who knowingly or recklessly makes any material false statement will be liable, on summary conviction, to imprisonment for a term not exceeding three months or to a fine not exceeding fifty pounds or to both such imprisonment and fine.)

(1) Name in full    CLARIDGE    ~~George~~ Edward George
(Surname first in BLOCK CAPITALS.)

(2) Home address in full    20 Council Houses, RAMSBURY, Wilts.

(3) Date of birth    Sept 2nd 1915    = *24*

I hereby apply, on the following grounds, for a postponement certificate :—
(STATE HERE THE GROUNDS FOR YOUR APPLICATION AND LENGTH OF POSTPONEMENT DESIRED)

This man is one of my Tractor drivers and can do almost any job on the farm.

He is my reserve milker.

I should like a postponement certificate for as long as possible.

NOTE.—If you wish, you may obtain at A on the back of this form a signed statement by another person in confirmation of the above.

Sign here    *R A Chamberlain*

Date    *Feb 19th 1940*

Date of receipt at L.O.

### FOR OFFICIAL USE.

*Applicant requested to call for interview on............by (Inits.)............(Date)............
*Questionnaire despatched to applicant on............by (Inits.)............(Date)............

Decision { *Liability postponed until (Date)............
*Refer to Military Service (Hardship) Committee.
*Application out of time—Dismissed.

Signature ............

Rank ............

N.S.64 issued............(Inits.)............(Date)............

Cause List. Sheet No.............Line No.............

N.S. 13.    * Delete inapplicable items.

---

**Left:** On 19th February 1940 Mr R A Chamberlain, a farmer from Ramsbury, applied to the Ministry of Labour for a postponement certificate for Mr Edward George Claridge of 20 Council Houses, Whittonditch Road, Ramsbury, who was one of his tractor drivers.

*I was in charge of all aspects of ploughing, sowing and harvesting, besides travelling around the district with a threshing machine. Therefore I was exempt from military service - I did try volunteering several times, but was always rejected".* When the call came for men to join the LDV Mr Edwards was one of the first to volunteer. *"I went to the local police station* [with several others] *to enrol where we were issued with an armband with LDV on it and also broom sticks and pick axe handles* [to use] *as weapons".*

As well as those employed in reserved occupations there were men from two other groups that would normally be found in a typical platoon. The first group were those aged 17-18 who were awaiting call-up. The lower age limit was not always strictly enforced and depended to a large extent upon where the applicant lived and which platoon he was trying to join. George Johnson who lived in Marlborough recalls, *"Jess Sandford went to join up but Sgt. Osgood knew he was only 15-years-old and told him he couldn't join and would have to wait. I was also 15 and they knew my age, but Major Parmenter* [No. 7 Platoon Commander] *lived next door to us in Barn Street. He also worked for A E Farr Construction at Wye House and my mother cleaned their offices - I think that's how I got in!"* John Bower also lived in Marlborough and at 16½ was still officially too young to join. He went along to enrol with his father and despite freely admitting his age was still signed up. *"We were given an armband marked LDV and I remember going up on the downs and all I had* [for protection] *was a blooming great stick!"*

The remaining group were men beyond call-up age and many were First World War veterans. John Bower recalls, *"These 'old boys' taught us a thing or two and I think we were a well trained and very efficient unit - when I went into the army in 1942 I was very good at square bashing."* Peter Piper was another young Marlborough recruit and remembers, *"There was a lot of enthusiasm generated by the 'old boys'. I was in Austin Ledley's platoon and the youngsters among us were named 'Ledley's Whippets'. During one Sunday morning exercise, and unbeknown to the older members of the platoon, we rode our bicycles to Barton copse on the Marlborough Downs and when the*

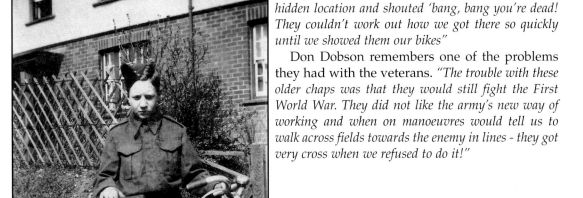

*rest of the platoon arrived we jumped out from our hidden location and shouted 'bang, bang you're dead! They couldn't work out how we got there so quickly until we showed them our bikes"*

Don Dobson remembers one of the problems they had with the veterans. *"The trouble with these older chaps was that they would still fight the First World War. They did not like the army's new way of working and when on manoeuvres would tell us to walk across fields towards the enemy in lines - they got very cross when we refused to do it!"*

**Left:** George Johnson was only 15-years-old when he joined the Home Guard and his youthful features are very evident in this photograph (George Johnson)

*Left and bottom left:* In civilian life William Bower was employed by the Automobile Association as a patrolman, and before the war covered the A4 between Marlborough and Beckhampton on a motor-cycle combination painted in the AA's distinctive yellow and black colour scheme.

By the summer of 1940, with petrol rationing beginning to bite, the number of civilian motorists had declined rapidly and the demands placed on AA patrols reduced accordingly. Initially, even the AA struggled to get sufficient amounts of petrol for its own use, and for awhile instructed its patrols to cover their beats on bicycles!

With patrolmen being called up in increasing numbers for military service, and the difficulty in obtaining petrol, the Association was forced to reduce its number of road patrols from a pre-war total of 2,500 to just 300.

Fortunately William Bower was one of the surviving patrols, and in addition to his pre-war equipment now had a tin hat, respirator and a camouflaged motorcycle. His new wartime duties kept him very busy and included the removal of AA road and direction signs - in case they should help an invading enemy - directing military convoys, and from 1943, erecting special signs to help newly arrived American troops find their way around Wiltshire's roads. (photographs via Mark Clements and John Bower)

*Right:* On 14th May 1940, following Anthony Eden's radio broadcast, William Bower and his son John were amongst the first to go along to Marlborough Town Hall and join the LDV. In 1944, when this picture was taken, he was a Sergeant in No 4 Platoon, A Company (John Robins)

# 6. Home Guard transport

Improvisation was the key word when it came to providing Home Guard units with a means of transportation. The authorities were hard pressed re-equipping the regular army to worry about the Home Guard, so the force had to do the best it could with whatever it could find.

Many of the Marlborough battalion's higher-ranking officers, such as its company and platoon commanders, were farmers or well paid professional people who owned motorcars, and some were prepared to use them for Home Guard business. In addition the battalion also included within its ranks a large number of motorcyclists, as well as tradesmen who owned and operated vans and lorries.

Wartime petrol rationing began in Britain on 16th September 1939 and as the war progressed it became more and more difficult for motorists to get petrol, and many private vehicles were laid up for the duration. However, as from 27th June 1940 personnel travelling on authorised Home Guard business of two miles or more had their petrol paid for, but they still had to surrender the required number of petrol coupons to get it!

By 1942 the price of wartime petrol had been set at 1/6d (7½p) per gallon, but the mileage allowance for Home Guard work varied according to the vehicle's Horsepower - for a car with an 8 Horsepower rating the allowance for the first 250 miles in any one calendar month was 4½d per mile. Claims for mileage allowance were countersigned by the unit or company commander and then forwarded to the Territorial Army Association for payment.

Nearly every platoon had at least one despatch rider, who usually got the job simply because he owned a motorcycle! It was also important that he knew the local area like the back of his hand and could read a map. George Cady lived in Burbage, but had joined the Durley section (later to become the Savernake Platoon) because he was friendly with Lionel Wootton who was second in command - in overall charge was the Marquis of Ailesbury. George recalls, *"I had a motorbike, so I was the despatch rider and used to go up to the Marquis of Ailesbury at Tottenham House*

***Above:*** Tommy Lunn ran a small garage and petrol filling station in West Street, Aldbourne. He also owned several Ford V8 motor cars and operated a car hire business. He loaned the platoon one of his vehicles and had it modified by applying a coat of camouflage paint and adding mountings for machine guns. The car is seen near the Four Barrows track and standing in front of the vehicle are, from left to right: Bill Price, Gerald Jerram, Les Stacey and Tommy Lunn (via Murray Maclean)

*with messages and over to Colonel Snow at Wilton"*. Len Richardson owned a BSA motorcycle and was Baydon's despatch rider. *"I was attached to the Army at Russley Park to deliver messages to the Home Guard. I used to come home from work, drain all the petrol out of my tank (leaving just enough to get to Russley Park) and the Army would then fill it up for me from flimsy two-gallon cans!"*

Jack Rickards was Avebury's village baker and he used a Ford 5cwt van to deliver bread around the district. Every other Saturday night he would go on OP duty at Windmill Hill and normally took the patrol up to the post in his van. On other nights Frank Cullis, who ran the garage in Avebury, would undertake the same task using one of his fleet of cars.

Don Dobson remembers that the local coalmen in Marlborough were asked to make their lorries available. *"In the event of an invasion alarm they were to collect us in their lorries and take us down to the Marlborough College armoury, which was just behind the memorial hall, and issue out the weapons"*. Frank Smith lived in the small village of Axford, which is a couple of miles west of Ramsbury, and owned a lorry that he used for haulage work. One Sunday morning Edward Wilson from Park Farm made contact and asked him to move some cattle from fields in the Kennet valley up to the farm. The farm was on the western edge of Ramsbury airfield and Frank had to drive his lorry across the airfield to get there. At that time the airfield was occupied by elements of the US 9th Air Force and as Frank approached the main gate he was stopped by guards, who asked to see his pass. Unfortunately he had not been given one, but managed to convince them that the only way he could get the cattle in his truck to Park Farm was via the airfield, and they let him through. For several more Sundays, using the same route, Frank moved cattle from the valley to Park Farm and the guards became so familiar with his regular comings and goings that after a while they waved him through without even looking in the lorry.

One Sunday morning an exercise had been organised between the US Forces stationed on the airfield and the Home Guard. As luck would have it Ramsbury's platoon commander was Edward Wilson whose objective was to get his men onto the airfield undetected and 'destroy' as many parked aircraft as possible. To satisfy the exercise umpires that the task had been completed each 'destroyed' plane had to be marked with a cross. Wilson quickly devised a plan and told Frank Smith that instead of picking up cattle he wanted him to drive his lorry to Ramsbury School. At the school a section from Wilson's platoon clambered aboard Frank's lorry, which then made its way to the airfield's main gate, as it had done every Sunday morning for the past few weeks. Frank was waved through as usual and quickly made his way over to a number of parked aircraft where the men jumped out and marked the planes with crosses. The Ramsbury Home Guard had easily and successfully completed the exercise outfoxing the Americans and no doubt leaving them with a lot of questions to answer.

**Left:** Three of Tommy Lunn's Ford cars lined up near the village pump in West Street. The upstairs room of the building on the left of the picture was Aldbourne's Home Guard Platoon Headquarters (via Murray Maclean)

**Right:** It was not unusual during the war for civilian or military police officers to stop motorists and check they had a legitimate reason for being on the road. On 10th July 1942, to prove that he was authorised to use a car on Home Guard business, Sergeant Tommy Lunn was issued this permit by Lt. Col. Fuller.

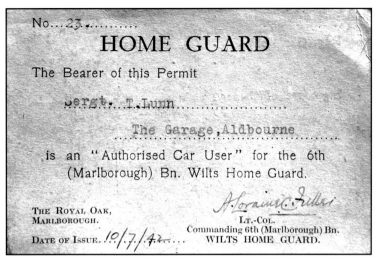

No...23...........

# HOME GUARD

The Bearer of this Permit

Serst...T.Lunn.....................

The Garage, Aldbourne

is an "Authorised Car User" for the 6th (Marlborough) Bn. Wilts Home Guard.

THE ROYAL OAK,
MARLBOROUGH.

LT.-COL.
Commanding 6th (Marlborough) Bn.
DATE OF ISSUE. 10/7/42..... WILTS HOME GUARD.

**Below:** Despite wartime petrol rationing Marlborough High Street could still buzz with traffic from time to time, as we can see from this picture. Many of the vehicles have military or commercial functions, but there are still a surprising number of private cars on the road. The odd looking structure in the foreground marked 'keep left' was a static water tank. There was a further example at the opposite end of the High Street and another on The Green. They were designed to hold between 10,000 and 15,000 gallons of water to help the National Fire Service quench fires in the event of an enemy air raid. (George Johnson)

# 7. Marlborough College & the Army Cadets

There has been a boarding school on the same site at Marlborough for more than 150 years, but one of the biggest upheavals in its long history occurred when the City of London School (CLS) was evacuated to the college just before the outbreak of World War Two.

As early as 1938 people were beginning to realise that war with Nazi Germany was unavoidable and the extensive buildings complex at Marlborough College would be perfect for accommodating students from evacuated schools in London. Rather than leave things to chance the CLS was approached and, in the event of war, invited to come to Marlborough College and share its facilities. On 1st September 1939 the inevitable evacuation from London began and on the same day boys from the CLS started arriving in Marlborough by train.

Like other public schools Marlborough had an Officer's Training Corps (OTC). It offered students basic military training and an opportunity to apply for a commission in the regular army, providing they successfully gained the OTC certificate - the certificate exempted them from sitting certain entrance examinations.

In May 1940, following Eden's announcement of the formation of the LDV, the OTC was asked to form its own unit, which would become part of the Marlborough Town Company (later 'A' Company). By July 1940 three platoons had been raised and most boys over the age of 17 had enrolled. One of the advantages the college platoons had over other LDV units was access to the OTC's .303 Lee Enfield rifles held in the college armoury. In the beginning each student was issued one round of .303 ammunition, but this was later increased to five rounds.

During the 1940 summer term the boys undertook duties near the college, such as manning roadblocks on the Bath road and at Cow bridge, but these were discontinued after awhile and replaced by standing patrols on high ground above Manton village and on the Manton Hollow road where there was an OP. Because the boys were young and fit they were eventually formed into mobile columns whose task was to chase enemy paratroopers dropped in the area! All this activity meant that on average boys spent one night in three on duty and Masters two nights in five. The long hours took their toll, particularly on Masters, and tiredness was a constant companion.

One of the Masters at the college was Arthur Raymond Pepin, who was very interested in the development of wireless. He had two huge wireless sets in his classroom, which he used to communicate with places all around the world. In 1934 he helped found the school's wireless society and two years later produced a 5-metre walkie-talkie set, the first of its kind. When the LDV was formed Pepin became the Marlborough Battalion's communication officer and laid miles of telephone wire all around the town linking important buildings within the anti-tank island. The battalion's HQs at the Royal Oak boasted its own signals room, which was frequently manned by college boys.

The college looked after a lot of 'A' Company's weapons, which were kept in the armoury, and an entry in the OTC's 1942 log book records that amongst other things it held 20 Spigot Mortars and 8 Northover Projectors - on Friday afternoons the students received training on these weapons. The log book also states that the college platoons were made responsible for the Fougasse. This statement proves the existence of at least one Fougasse in Marlborough, but gives no clue to its location.

# Army Cadet Force

**Aldbourne Platoon, Army Cadet Force (6th Wilts)**
*Picture taken at the Old Manor, Aldbourne in 1944 (via C. Cowles)*
G. Chamberlain
F. Wilkins, S. Barrett, D. Barrett, T. Barnes, C. Cowles, H. Wilkins
D. Keen, J. Barnes, P. Hall, P. Smyth, J. Wootton, T. Halkins
P. Haines (seated left), C. Brown - instructor (centre), C. Palmer (seated right)

The Army Cadet Force (ACF) was a nationwide organisation created in 1942 and open to boy's aged 14-17. Initially about 150 lads from the Marlborough district enrolled. From the very beginning there were close links between the ACF and the Home Guard, as local platoons would often provide the boys with a tutor. The picture above emphasises this fact, as Mr C Brown, the Aldbourne Cadet Force instructor, was also a sergeant in the Home Guard. The aim of the ACF was to prepare the cadets for army service by sitting the army's qualification 'A' certificate - once qualified they were allowed to participate in certain Home Guard activities.

Two platoons were formed in Marlborough both run by Major Shaw. They were named Grammar School Platoon and Town Platoon and their first parade took place on 19th March 1942.

At the age of 15 Reg Perry joined the Army Cadets and remembers working closely with the Burbage Home Guard. In charge was Bernard Ford, a local solicitor, and their HQ was the village hall at Stibb Green (now demolished). On the downs at South Grove was an old shepherds hut that was used as an observation post - should German paratroops land in the area those on duty in the hut had orders to ride their bicycles into Burbage and warn the village! On Sunday mornings the platoon was taken by army lorry for rifle practice at the ranges between

Tidworth and Bulford. Reg was only 4 feet 11 inches tall, weighed just 8½ stone and had great difficulty carrying his rifle - when firing the gun on the ranges its kick always bruised his shoulder.

Alf Exell was a member of Baydon's ACF and clearly remembers the night of October 14th 1943 when an American B-17 bomber crashed near the village. *"I was in the Army Cadet Force and we were often called out, jointly with the Home Guard, to incidents in our area. I remember it was after dark but there must have been a moon because we had no difficulty finding our way around. We were told that a plane had crashed just to the southeast of the village and we made our way along a track which heads out of Baydon towards Marridge Hill. After we'd been marching for about half-a-mile we came to Gore's Copse and close by were the remains of a Flying Fortress. We were hoping to find a few souvenirs - perhaps even a leather flight jacket - but US service personnel had already arrived on the scene and kept us well away"*.

During the war 'Mac' McKechnie lived at Avington, a small Berkshire hamlet a couple of miles east of Hungerford. 'Mac' wanted to join the ACF but as no unit existed in Hungerford he and many other boys from the town had to cross the county boundary into Wiltshire and join the Chilton Foliat cadets. *"We used the old mill building as our headquarters often sharing it with the Home Guard - rifles and equipment were stored there. I believe the man in charge of us was called Lanfear, who had been a Sergeant in the Wiltshire Regiment and was quite an elderly gentleman. We did a lot of training with the Home Guard all around the village including Littlecote Park and also at Marlborough College"*. The Chilton Foliat Cadets took part in many parades including Hungerford's 'Wings for Victory' and 'Salute the Soldier' weeks.

The cadets were supplied with standard army battledress uniforms, side caps, anklets and boots. They wore the Wiltshire Regiment cap badge and had shoulder titles marked 'Army Cadet' stitched to their uniforms. In addition they also had a specially designed county patch made from a square of light blue material which was worn on the left sleeve of the battledress blouse. Printed on the patch was the outline of a prehistoric trilithon (two upright stones capped with a stone lintel) and two crossed rakes all superimposed on a yellow moon - the trilithon symbolised Stonehenge, Wiltshire's most famous icon, and the moon and rakes represented the expression 'Moonraker' a name given to people born in the county and derived from a local legend. The Marlborough area cadets collectively formed the 6th Wilts ACF and to signify this fact wore a patch of khaki material printed with a black six on their right sleeve.

 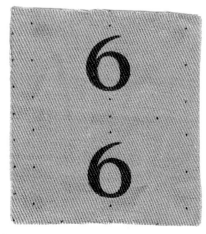

On the left is the Wiltshire ACF county badge and on the right the 6th Wilts ACF designation. The latter was printed on a roll of khaki coloured material, which was cut into paired numbers before being handed to the cadets.

# 8. *Training, training and more training*

On 22nd June 1941 Hitler surprised the world by launching operation 'Barbarossa' - the invasion of Russia. His armies made swift and decisive progress along a 500 mile front and Russian losses were staggering. In Britain this was initially viewed as great news, as Hitler's armies were now fighting on two fronts and Britain had a new ally. However, as the Germans rapidly advanced eastwards there was a very real possibility that Russian resistance would collapse completely or, in desperation, Stalin would negotiate some sort of deal. Either way Hitler would be in a position once again to turn his attention fully towards Britain.

With this in mind it was vitally important that the Home Guard remained vigilant and continued its preparations to repel an invasion. From 1941 onwards its emphasis shifted towards training with an ever increasing number of large and realistic exercises. To help keep the Home Guard's spirit alive the War Office issued a wealth of instruction leaflets and manuals, produced training films, ran courses and put on demonstrations.

Most units held an evening meeting during the middle of the week at their platoon HQs and these were often reserved for lectures on subjects such as fieldcraft, the care and maintenance of weapons or how to disable an enemy tank. On Sundays the platoons would meet on open spaces such as village greens and recreation fields or in their platoon commander's garden to try and put the theory into practice.

The following is part of an amusing poem written by Sergeant Ronald Robins from Marlborough in which he describes his platoon going off on a training exercise.

**'Tactical operations by the Home Guard'**
I belong to Four Platoon,
Who march in step and sing in tune.
The NCOs are in the van,
With me in the rear an also ran.

Marching down the wide High Street,
Tin hats on head and iron shod feet.
Marching on with steady gait,
Round Bernard's corner at a hell of a rate.

Soon we reach the college slope,
A traffic jam is my only hope.
Swinging right through the Barton mire,
Gaiters all splashed, I curse and perspire.

Steadily on through the old farm yard,
Where the grounds all muck and the goings hard.
Soon we reach the Barton copse, startle a hare,
And I think it's the wops.

The parades or exercises often ended at the local pub, as 'Tiny' Watts recalls. *"I was in Jack Watts section together with Walt Dyer and Harry Watts. Jack and Walt lived at Marridge Hill and I lived at Balak. When we went on parade Jack provided the transport and we always picked up Harry at the Crown and Anchor* [in Ramsbury]. *The Crown and Anchor featured large in the Sunday parades as we adjourned there afterwards to drink to Hitler's downfall! I recall one Sunday after a few pints we went round to the downs behind Preston and put up some targets, as Ted Watts had got hold of a box of ammunition - this was very unofficial. We started to blast away at the targets with great glee, only to have to abandon our fun and beat out the burning grass - all the ammunition was tracer!"*

On Sunday mornings the East Grafton Platoon normally fell in at about 9:30 in front of the Swan Inn at Wilton. Two-and-a-half-hours later Lieutenant Dick Margesson, the platoon's commander, usually managed to bring proceedings to an end in exactly the same place! Bill Eastmond recalls, *"Dick Margesson was a really nice man and he would always buy everybody a pint, as did Sgt. Mundy. So after the parade we would have one or two pints, without paying, and then cycle home for dinner!"*

During early 1941, as part of a Sunday morning exercise, 'A' Company had to attack and capture the village of Aldbourne. *"We were taken out in lorries and dropped off near Aldbourne Warren"*, recalls John Bower. *"The company then had to walk into the village using fields on either side of the Swindon road. The Aldbourne Platoon was hidden in various places near Brown's Farm to protect the village. We had to approach in a stealthy manner, but when we 'fired' our rifles had to shout 'bang' because we didn't have any blank ammunition! After the exercise everybody adjourned to the pub and then we were taken back to Marlborough in the trucks that had brought us."*

The Mildenhall Road Platoon, part of 'A' Company, set up its HQs in the Queen's Head public house in St Martins, as 'Eddy' Witts recalls. *"We usually had a Sunday morning parade of some sort and would drill on the college fields or have an exercise along Treacle Bolly. Afterwards it was back to the Queen's Head and I would have a lemonade, as I hadn't got the taste for beer then"*. Peter Piper enjoyed drinking beer, but was too young to enter a pub. *"When Sunday exercise was over we would all go back to the pub for a pint and our lot drank in the Royal Oak* [Battalion HQs]. *Some of us were not old enough to drink, but on the right of the Royal Oak was an arch (now filled in) and someone would usually bring us out a pint and we'd drink it there"*.

**Rifle Ranges**

Most platoons had access to a rifle range although they often had to share facilities with neighbouring units. For example men from Aldbourne and Baydon had to travel to Windmill Farm, which was just over the county boundary in Berkshire, to use the Lambourn Company's range. *"We used to go there most Sunday mornings"*, recalls Len Richardson. *"I remember Walter Hall on the range. I was down in the trench in front of the targets and you would receive a signal to get down when they started firing. Walter Hall missed the target by about two yards and sent chalk all down my neck! We had a pole with a red disk on one end to show where the bullet had hit the target - we called it a tomato. I was a good shot and had a silver spoon presented for shooting"*.

'A' Company used the Marlborough College range at Rough Down, known as the Butts, which was in the valley on the eastern side of the Rockley road just to the north of Marlborough common. Peter Piper and Eric Jones were put in charge of a Lewis gun and on occasions actually fired it at the Butts. Peter Piper remembers there were numerous firing points laid back from the target at intervals of 100 yards or so.

Just like Len Richardson, George Johnson also spent time in front of the target holding up markers to indicate which part had been hit. *"One day when we were in the pit we got the fags out. Somebody soon appeared and told us to put the cigarettes out because the smoke was blinding the target!"* One First World War veteran, who was in the same platoon as Don Dobson, was an excellent shot. *"Corporal Cannings, who worked at the college, was a really good shot"*, recalls Don.

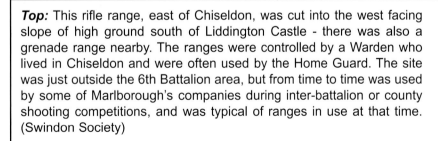

**Top:** This rifle range, east of Chiseldon, was cut into the west facing slope of high ground south of Liddington Castle - there was also a grenade range nearby. The ranges were controlled by a Warden who lived in Chiseldon and were often used by the Home Guard. The site was just outside the 6th Battalion area, but from time to time was used by some of Marlborough's companies during inter-battalion or county shooting competitions, and was typical of ranges in use at that time. (Swindon Society)

**Above:** The view eastwards towards the butts clearly showing all 12 range targets. (Swindon Society)

**Left:** Teaspoons, like the one shown here, were typically given as prizes to successful competitors at Home Guard shooting competitions.

*"He was an old chap and never said very much. When we were on the rifle range he would lie down and gee wiz you could tell he'd been in the First World War, because time after time, no matter what the distance, he'd get that bullet on the bull. We had shooting competitions and he'd win everything".*

## Battle Schools

When vacancies occurred officers from the battalion were sent on three-day courses to Denbies near Dorking, Surrey, which was one of several national centres run by the War Office to train the Home Guard. To further assist with training travelling wings were periodically sent out from these centres and eventually all of the UK's Home Guard Battalions were visited at least once. Each wing consisted of Officers, Warrant Officers and NCOs who were specialists in all aspects of warfare and during the early part of 1942 a wing, under the command of a Captain Merrick, visited Marlborough.

At a local level the first attempt at centralised training was made during the early part of 1941 when the 7th (Salisbury) Battalion ran a series of very successful three-day courses at Bulford Camp. Salisbury Plain Area (SPA) soon established its own permanent Home Guard School at the camp and periodically officers and men from the Marlborough Battalion would be sent there on weekend courses. Saturdays were usually reserved for classroom lectures and on Sundays lessons learned were put into practice.

During the First World War an airfield was constructed on land just to the west of Stonehenge. Its workshops, accommodation huts and hangars were built either side of the Amesbury-Exeter road (A303) and the landing area was a triangular field bounded by the A303, A344 and A360. The airfield became operational in October 1917 and its purpose was to train bomber pilots in both day and night flying roles. So that pilots on night training could sleep during the day a separate camp was built away from the noise of the airfield on the northern side of the A344 near Fargo plantation.

The airfield closed in 1921 and by 1930 all of its buildings, with the exception of those at Fargo plantation, had been removed. By 1942 the remaining structures had been taken over by the SPA Home Guard school and converted into a mock village where practical exercises, including live firing, could take place. An old tank, probably recovered from the gunnery ranges at Larkhill, was used as a practice target for live bombs and grenades.

Over the weekend of 22nd/23rd August 1942 Lieutenant William Young attended a course at the school. The weather on the 22nd was poor but Sunday dawned bright and sunny with a refreshing breeze blowing across the plain. At 08:00hrs Young and the rest of his course

## OSTERLEY PARK TRAINING SCHOOL

THE Osterley Training School is situated inside the estate of Osterley Park, kindly lent by Lord Jersey, which is about 9 miles west of London, just off the Great West Road. It can be reached by underground to Osterley Station (Piccadilly Line, 30 minutes from Piccadilly).

### THE PURPOSE OF THE SCHOOL

The Training School exists for the benefit of the Home Guard, to provide a quick course in certain aspects of modern war. It is staffed by a group of men with knowledge and experience of modern warfare, in France, Flanders, India, Spain and elsewhere. It is under the general direction of Tom Wintringham, whose articles in *Picture Post*, the *Daily Mirror* and elsewhere are well-known, and who has been lecturing to the army at War Office request.

The School does not teach drill, which can readily be learned elsewhere. Its aim is to give the largest amount of serviceable information, directly related to the conditions of present-day fighting, in the shortest possible amount of time, and to teach it in such a way that those who take the course will be able to pass on what they have learnt to their own detachment. It is hoped that many Home Guard Units will choose two or three representatives to attend the course on their behalf.

### LENGTH OF TRAINING COURSE

Each course lasts for two days, and there are three two-day courses every week. Monday-Tuesday; Wednesday-Thursday; Friday-Saturday. The hours are from 9 a.m. to 6 p.m. each day, and they will be kept to strictly. Applicants for the course must apply at headquarters (near the training grounds) *before* 9 a.m.; they must be prepared to turn up promptly on each of the two days and to remain until the course is complete.

The capacity of the school is about 60 trainees at a time.

Application must be made in writing at least four days in advance. No guarantee can be given to provide instruction for any who have not applied and received notice of acceptance in advance. Trainees should go straight to the headquarters of the School, at 72 Bassett Gardens, Osterley, Middlesex, where they should register with the Officer in Charge.

### LIVING ARRANGEMENTS AND EQUIPMENT

The course, for the present, is free. Applicants will be responsible for making their own arrangements about accommodation. But the Officer in Charge will do his best to find space under camping conditions for those who write to him at least a week in advance. Blankets and emergency rations must be brought.

There is a marquee inside the grounds for instruction on wet days.

Anyone who has a steel helmet, rifle or other weapon should bring it with him. Gas masks must be brought. It is suggested that trainees who have not yet got uniform should wear their oldest clothes and bring an old raincoat with them.

*All communications should be sent to headquarters, addressed to the Officer in Charge.*

**Left:** Osterley Park is a large mansion situated in the London Borough of Hounslow. During the summer of 1940 the Home Guard's first training school was privately established in its grounds by writer Captain Tom Wintringham. Copies of this leaflet were sent out to Home Guard units throughout the country encouraging members to take part in the school's two day courses. Unfortunately the War Office was unhappy with Wintringham's unorthodox methods and alleged left wing tendencies and took control of the school in September 1940, closing it the following year. New War Office approved schools were then set up around the country.

left Bulford in army vehicles and made their way to the mock village via Amesbury. Young was very impressed with the village and thought it was an excellent place for street fighting demonstrations and practice. During the morning the platoon had a demonstration in Fargo plantation of how best to clear enemy troops from woodland, followed by a very realistic street fighting exercise. Then came tank hunting and destruction - the old tank was hit by various types of high explosives and set ablaze. After lunch Young was put in charge of the group and set the task of attacking in sections an isolated body of troops some distance south of Fargo plantation near Lake Down. After the exercise everybody came in for a degree of sharp criticism from a Major with a monocle! Young had thoroughly enjoyed the day but was just about ready to drop by the time he boarded the bus that took the course back to Bulford. At 19:00hrs, after listening to the final summing up, Young left Bulford and an hour later arrived in Marlborough where Major Giffard was waiting to take him back to Avebury.

## Major exercises

As the Home Guard became more proficient major exercises of one sort or another started to dominate its training. Many of these were mock battles and platoons would 'fight' other local platoons, or regular army units that were stationed nearby. The following are some of the larger exercises in which the Marlborough Battalion participated.

**Marlborough Civil Defence exercise, 15th February 1942**

Like the majority of exercises it took place on a Sunday when most participants were free of work commitments. As its name implies it was more of a civil defence exercise than a military one, but the Home Guard was still expected to play its part. Some of the exercise objectives were to encourage closer co-operation between the civil and military organisations, fire fighting, handling casualties and keeping the general public informed about what was going on.

The exercise started at 9:00am and shortly afterwards the Home Guard was ordered to disrupt petrol supplies - as this was an exercise they simply checked that arrangements were in place. At 9:30am checkpoints were manned and as the day progressed mock paratroop landings and bombing raids took place across the region. In Ramsbury serious fires had supposedly taken hold and five civilians and five Home Guards were wounded. George Edwards from Ramsbury remembers one exercise he took part in. *"It was the middle of winter and very cold and some of our men were supposed to be casualties. One man lay beside the road for about three hours. No one came to attend to him, so he got up, knocked on the door of the house opposite, asked for a piece of chalk and wrote on the pavement 'Bled to death, gone home!'"*

At 11:00am Home Guard units made contact with German forces, which were approaching Marlborough from the direction of Savernake, and in Froxfield it was reported that tanks were in action near Hungerford and moving westwards. The Chilton Foliat platoon had engaged the tanks and four of its men had been killed, six wounded and two taken prisoner.

The exercise was timed to end at 12:15pm when it was hoped that at least half the roadblocks in the region would be in position and manned. No doubt once the exercise was over many of its participants retired to the local pub for a well earned pint!

The following is an excerpt from a letter written during 1942 by Chris L Lovell, a student at Marlborough College, and describes what it was like to be a casualty on a Home Guard exercise. It is reproduced by the kind permission of the Marlborough College Archive.

*"I volunteered with some other boys to be a casualty for a Home Guard exercise. We changed into games clothes before breakfast on Sunday morning and went to wait for cars to take us to our destination, a dilapidated house.*

# INVASION EXERCISE

## MARLBOROUGH

THIS exercise has been arranged for SUNDAY, 31ST JANUARY, 1943, between the hours of 8.30 and 5 o'clock and will be the biggest of the kind attempted in Marlborough. May I take the opportunity of emphasising the following points affecting the people of Marlborough as a whole?

Households living within 60—70 yards of Road Blocks are asked to make their contribution to the realism of the exercise by being ready to evacuate temporarily if required to do so. This does not mean that Military or Civil Defence Forces will enter the house or that everyone is expected to move out. But it is hoped that at any rate one person in each house (where there are more than this number) will be willing to come out, so that the W.V.S. can practice their arrangements for emergency feeding.

Those who move will be given a mid-day meal and will be told where to go when evacuated. They must not forget to take identity cards, gas masks, overcoats, and a blanket.

Everybody in the Borough should be ready to play their part in the exercise in the following ways:—

(a) To assist the Military and Civil Defence Forces to the utmost and to take part in incidents in their streets.
(b) To be ready to take into their houses temporarily people who have been evacuated.
(c) To keep off the streets when fighting is taking place in the Town and to avoid at all times standing about in groups.
(d) To keep in touch with the nearest Warden or Housewife.
(e) To refuse information to the enemy if interrogated.
(f) To rely for information on the Official Notice Boards at the following places:—

TOWN HALL
NATIONAL FIRE SERVICE DEPOT, LONDON ROAD
MARLBOROUGH COLLEGE
ST. PETER'S CHURCH
ST. THOMAS MORE R.C. CHURCH, ELCOT LANE.

\* \* \* \* \*

The Exercise should not interfere with the normal Services at the various Places of Worship in the Town.

Yours faithfully,
F. J. HARRAWAY,
Chairman of Invasion Committee,
Borough of Marlborough.

N.B.—All BRITISH Forces will be wearing STEEL HELMETS. All "ENEMY" Soft Hats. All TANKS will be treated as "ENEMY."

1, The Green, Marlborough, Wilts,
January 28th, 1943.

**Left:** 'Royal Oak' was the largest invasion exercise to take place in Marlborough during WWII and to ensure that the people of the town knew exactly what was going on every household received a copy of this leaflet. (John Robins)

**Below:** This picture, dated 1941, was taken near the Castle and Ball in Marlborough High Street and shows Sgt Joseph Frank Biggs waiting, along with other members of his platoon, for a parade or exercise to begin. (Mrs Margaret Wharton)

**Above:** This message form was used by Marlborough's No. 4 Platoon during a Home Guard exercise. (John Robins)

*Once there we were given labels to tie on to ourselves stating what was supposed to be wrong. I was to lie on the ground and to foam at the mouth and we all had to distribute ourselves round the house. I went into the basement and put a piece of barbed wire in the window to make it more difficult for the rescuers. Eventually the rescue squad and the ambulance men arrived. One boy was meant to be gassed, but they did not know what to do with him and I heard the casualty suggest that they give him artificial respiration!*

*At last I was discovered by two men who became totally entangled in my barbed wire. They spent most of the next 15 minutes trying to extricate themselves from the wire and in futile shouts for a stretcher. Eventually one climbed out and returned with the news that all the stretchers were in use and that we would have to wait for an ambulance to return some! When, eventually, the stretcher arrived they were unable to lift me on to it, so I had to get on it myself! They tried to carry me out, but one of the men slipped and fell on the wire, and I rolled off the stretcher as he let go. I climbed back on, and they started again and actually progressed a few feet before they stopped to allow the front two men to climb through the window. Then, with the two men inside pushing and the two outside pulling, there was a sudden crack as one of the handles of the stretcher hit the side of the window, bringing down about 10 bricks! Shortly thereafter, as the last two men climbed out there was another avalanche of bricks as the tin hat of one of them hit the top of the window!*

*At last they got me out and along came a man who read my label and wrote 'EPILEPTIC FIT' on the back of it. 'I hope you have treated him very gently' said he. 'Oh, yes said the man who had dropped me!*

*Eventually they got us to Savernake Hospital and the stretchers had just been unchained when the furniture van (for that is what the 'ambulance' really was) started to move and the nurse jumped out and ran for help. By the time she and the stretcher bearers returned we had stopped moving. The nurse asked why the brakes had not been put on. 'They were, but they hardly ever worked!' was the reply.*

*After pushing and shoving the stretchers bearers got me out of the van at last and into the hospital, where I was plonked on the floor. Two nurses seemed tremendously excited by my arrival, thinking that I had a fractured skull despite my label specifying that I was an epileptic!*

*In due course, we all rose from our stretchers and were getting ready to walk back to College when a nurse came in and told us that we couldn't leave as the exercise was still going on and the Home Guard was fighting outside. Accordingly, they gave us a wonderful lunch of roast pork, before letting us go. We saw little 'fighting' on the way back and what we did see seemed devoid of any purpose! We returned to an empty College and learned that all the others were cooped up in shelters as part of the exercise and that our house was supposed to have been burned to the ground. However, we still had hot baths and all of us casualties decided that being one wasn't so bad after all!"*

## Exercise 'Royal Oak'

This was the largest civil defence exercise ever to take place in Marlborough and was held on 31st January 1943. Its objective was to contain an attack by small parties of German paratroopers attempting to enter the town following an invasion. The German troops were portrayed by two squadrons of the RAF Regiment, two troops of tanks from 20th Armoured Brigade and 'D' Company, Marlborough Home Guard. The British side was represented by HQs, 'A' and 'E' Companies, Marlborough Home Guard, plus all civil defence services. To differentiate between friend and foe the 'Germans' wore field service caps and the 'British' steel helmets. Thunderflashes were used to represent bombs, mortars and grenades and to replicate fires and smoke screens, smoke generators were employed. For the final authentic touch 4,000 rounds of blank ammunition was distributed amongst those carrying revolvers, rifles and machine guns.

William Young from Avebury, together with four other officers from the battalion, were to act as umpires and on the Friday before the exercise attended a conference at the Town Hall. On the day of the exercise Young was supposed to watch activity around the defensive positions near The Green, but one of the other umpires, Lieutenant Horton from Winterbourne Bassett, failed to arrive on time and Young was sent off to Rabley Wood with 'A' Company instead.

'Royal Oak' was an all day exercise starting at 8:30am and finishing eight-and-a-half hours later. It followed a similar narrative to other exercises with 'enemy' troops approaching the town from various directions, imaginary air raids starting fires and reports of paratroopers being dropped around the town.

The reason for Lieutenant Horton's late arrival was because the Rockley road was blocked with trees that had been blown down during a gale the previous night. The weather throughout the exercise was terrible with high winds and heavy rain, but despite these problems 'Royal Oak' was considered a successful and worthwhile experience.

### Exercise 'White Horse'

By the late summer of 1943 preparations were underway for an allied invasion of northwest Europe and the War Office was beginning to think about what it should do if the Germans tried to disrupt its build-up. Exercise 'White Horse', which took place on 18th September 1943, was an attempt to prepare the Home Guard for such an eventuality.

Nine months later, during the real invasion period, the allies were still worried by the prospect of German interference and the Home Guard was called out to man strategic road and railway junctions. No doubt some of the lessons learned on 'White Horse' were put to good use during the real thing.

George Edwards took part in many Home Guard exercises and is pictured in uniform in his garden at Ramsbury with a P17 rifle and fixed bayonet. (Mrs Carol Silk)

# Certificate of Proficiency
## HOME GUARD

A.F.W 4026.

On arrival at the Training Establishment, Primary Training Centre or Recruit Training Centre, the holder must produce this Certificate at once for the officer commanding, together with Certificate A if gained in the Junior Training Corps or Army Cadet Force.

PART I. **I hereby certify** that (Rank) *Pte* (Name and initials) *R.R.L.Bush* Regiment HOME GUARD has qualified of *B* Battery *6th. WILTS. MARLBOROUGH BN.* Battalion of Company in the Proficiency Badge tests as laid down in the pamphlet "Qualifications for, and Conditions governing the Award of the Home Guard Proficiency Badges and Certificates" for the following subjects :—

| Subject | Date | Initials |
|---|---|---|
| 1. General knowledge (all candidates) | *16.2.44* | |
| 2. Rifle | | |
| 3. 36 M Grenade | | |
| *4. (a) Other weapon *S.E.* | | *060* |
| (b) Signalling | | |
| *5. (a) Battlecraft, (b) Coast Artillery, (c) Heavy A.A. Bty. work, (d) "Z" A.A. Battery work, (e) Bomb Disposal, (f) Watermanship, (g) M.T. | | |
| *6. (a) Map Reading, (b) Field works, (c) First Aid | | |

Date *17. Feb.* 194*4*     Signature *A.E.Norton maj*   • *President or Member of the Board.*

Date 194     Signature   • *President or Member of the Board.*

Date 194     Signature   • *President or Member of the Board.*

Date 194     Signature   • *President or Member of the Board.*

Date 194     Signature   • *President or Member of the Board.*

PART II. **I certify** that (Rank) *Pte* (Name and initials) *R.R.L.Bush* Regiment HOME GUARD, having duly passed of *B* Battery *6th. WILTS. MARLBOROUGH* Battalion the Proficiency tests in the subjects detailed above in accordance with the pamphlet and is hereby Company authorized to wear the Proficiency Badge as laid down in Regulations for the Home Guard, Vol. I, 1942, para. 41d.     Signature *Walter Giffard Lt.Col.*

Date *17 Feb.* 194*4*     Commanding *6th. WILTS MARLBOROUGH BN. H.G.* H.G.

PART III. If the holder joins H.M. Forces, his Company or equivalent Comm[...] particulars which he considers useful in assessing the man's value o[...] R.T.C., e.g. service, rank, duties on which employed, power of leader[...]

Date 194     Signature O.C[...]
• *Delete where not applicable.*

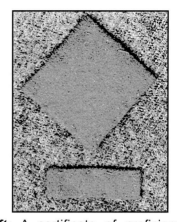

**Left:** A certificate of proficiency awarded to Private R R L Bush of Avebury Platoon. Accompanying the certificate was a red felt diamond and bar (above) and a note (below) from Lieutenant William Young, his platoon commander, instructing him to wear the badge five inches from the bottom of his right sleeve.

To:-   Pte. R.R.L.Bush,      As from "B" COY. OFFICE,
     No.4.Platoon.             MANOR BUNGALOW,
                               AVEBURY,
From:- O.C. "B" Coy., 6th Bn. Wilts H.G.    NR MARLBOROUGH.
                                     March 1st, 1944.
--------------------------------------------------------------

       I am forwarding your Certificate of Proficiency signed by Lt-Col. Giffard, and your Proficiency Badge, a red diamond with bar underneath, to be worn 5 inches from the bottom of the right sleeve.

       Please accept my hearty congratulations on your success.

                                 *W.E.F.Young* Lieut;
                                       for Major;
                 O.C. "B" Coy., 6th Bn. Wilts H.G.

*Notified in A.C.Is 19th May, 1943.*

NOT TO BE PUBLISHED
The information given in this document is not to be communicated, either directly or indirectly, to the Press or to any person not holding an official position in His Majesty's Service.

QUALIFICATIONS FOR, AND CONDITIONS GOVERNING THE AWARD OF THE HOME GUARD PROFICIENCY BADGES AND CERTIFICATES
1943

CONTENTS
PART I
General

Prepared under the direction of the Chief of the Imperial General Staff

THE WAR OFFICE,
19th May, 1943.

**HOME GUARD PROFICIENCY**
By
**JOHN BROPHY**

100 PRACTICAL QUESTIONS — WITH ANSWERS : PROBLEMS OF STRATEGY AND TACTICS : THE NORTHOVER : THE S.T. GRENADE : THE "THERMOS" ANTI-TANK GRENADE : GERMAN RIFLES, SUB-MACHINE GUNS, AUTOMATIC PISTOLS, HAND GRENADES

DIAGRAMS AND DETAILS.     124 PAGES

HODDER & STOUGHTON LIMITED    1/6 net

The need for some sort of award to show that members of the Home Guard had received official training was first mooted during late 1940, but it was April 1941 before the issue of a proficiency badge and certificate was approved. Official instructions were quickly produced governing the conditions of the award (far left) and a number of privately published booklets (like the example on the left by John Brophy), giving hints and tips on how to pass proficiency tests, soon appeared on the shelves of local bookshops.

# 9. The final years

A dark cloud hung over the opening months of 1943 because Lt. Col. Fuller had decided to move away from the area and consequently had to resign as commanding officer of the 6th Battalion. He had been in charge from the very beginning and was well respected and liked by most who knew him, as is evident from the following quote taken at the time from a local newspaper. *"He will indeed prove hard to replace, and, if it were not for the outstanding work that he has accomplished, replacement might have proved almost impossible"*. On 8th March 1943 the 6th Battalion organised a farewell dinner at the Royal Oak in his honour. Most of the battalion's senior officers were present and they all signed a specially designed souvenir card.

Major Giffard, 'B' Company's CO, took over from him in an acting capacity on 9th March, but was later promoted to Lt. Col. and given full command of the battalion. His place at 'B' Company was taken by Captain Dyball who was promoted to Major. Independently of the rest of the battalion, and as a mark of their affection for Lt. Col. Fuller, 'B' Company clubbed together and bought him a silver tankard and ash trays as well as presenting him with a magnificent signed scroll.

**Home Guard Anniversaries**

Each year, at around the anniversary time of the Home Guard's formation, some sort of parade and demonstration, usually involving entire battalions, took place in towns and cities all across the country and the 3rd anniversary in 1943 was no exception. The weather on Sunday 16th May was perfect for such an occasion and in Marlborough the Battalion, after forming up on the common, marched down past the Town Hall and into the High Street. Hundreds of local people lined the streets and a band played as the men marched past General Gathorne-Hardy who was standing outside the Royal Oak and took the salute. Later 'A' Company gave a battle drill demonstration at Barton Bottom.

Unfortunately the Home Guard's 4th anniversary celebration the following year proved to be a less auspicious occasion, for several reasons. At the beginning of 1942 the force stopped being a volunteer organisation when conscription was introduced. This move caused a lot of resentment throughout the Home Guard and morale suffered accordingly. By 1944 things had not improved significantly, absenteeism was becoming a problem and there was little appetite for organising anniversary parades with all the extra work they entailed. It must also be remembered that during the spring of 1944 the whole of the country's energies were being focused towards D-Day, the long awaited allied invasion of northwest Europe, and there was a very real possibility that the anniversary date would clash with this massively important operation.

Serious thought was given to abandoning the anniversary celebrations or postponing them until later in the year, but this idea would have almost certainly damaged morale further and it was decided to go ahead and the date was set for Sunday 4th June.

The march through the town was very different from the previous event, as only 'A' Company and the drill competing squads from the rest of the battalion took part. However, they were joined by all of the civil defence services plus a large contingent of US troops. Once again

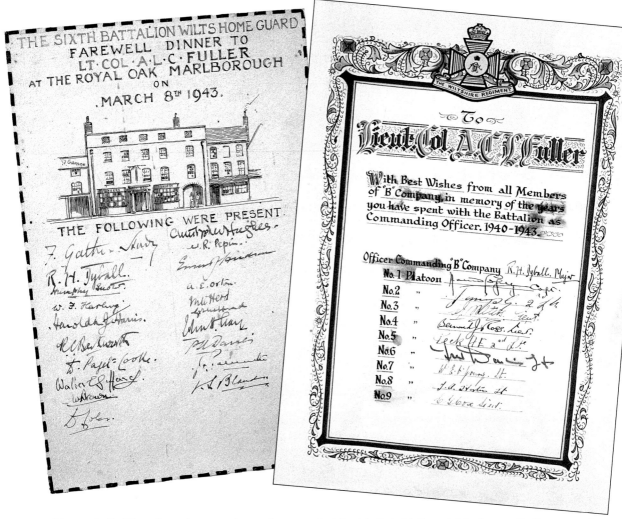

*Above left:* The signed souvenir card presented to Lt Col. Fuller at his farewell dinner and, *above right,* the beautiful scroll given by members of 'B' Company. (Mrs 'Vee' Fraser)
*Below:* One of many cards sent by Lt. Col. Fuller to men of his battalion - Christmas 1942.

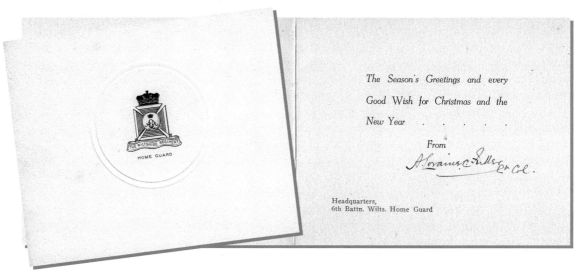

hundreds of civilians lined the streets to watch and they were not disappointed, as the procession included tanks, armoured cars and guns, plus tractors driven by girls from the Women's Land Army. An RAF band played rousing marches and it took some considerable time for the entire procession to pass the saluting base.

After the main part of the ceremony was over the various units dispersed, but the Home Guard marched to the Marlborough Town football field where representative platoons from each company took part in drill and tug-of-war competitions. The drilling was won by Aldbourne platoon who were presented with the 'Skurry Cup' for their efforts, and Avebury successfully beat off the opposition to win the tug-of-war - their victory was attributed to their superior weight.

Two days later, on 6th June, the newspapers and radio were full of reports and stories about the allies' successful landings on the Normandy beaches of France. Suddenly the reason why so many platoons had been absent from the weekend's celebrations became apparent. In the weeks leading up to D-Day they had been given instructions to guard bridges, crossings, junctions and stations on all of the railways in their area, as it was feared that German paratroops might attempt to disrupt the allies' invasion plans by targeting Britain's railway network.

At last, after several years of continuous training with little to show for it, the Home Guard had something worthwhile to get their teeth into and battalion and company HQs were manned 24 hours a day, with guarding continuing until 21st June. *"Over the D-Day period my platoon* [Little Bedwyn] *did certain duties down at Savernake Junction,"* recalls William Gauntlett. *"I cannot remember very much about it as I did not stay with them. Having accompanied some of the platoon to Savernake I had to return home to be near the telephone and keep in touch with the rest of my unit - I still had men on duty in the village watching for invasion. There was a lot of war material being moved to the south coast and all the Home Guard units from the Savernake Forest area were sent to do night duty around Savernake Railway Junction. I think my unit used to do about two nights a week. It was a very hard time for them after a long day of farm work, especially for men who had been in WWI so were 40 or 50 years old. Some of my men had to go straight from Home Guard night duty to milking and then do a days work after that. No leave in those days for farm workers!"*

Ray Beasley spent a lot of time at Savernake during this period and recalls. *"We spent two hours on and two hours off and had a 'Bell' tent where we could rest - sometimes we would lay on our overcoats and doze outside until it was our turn to go on duty again."*

**Stand Down**

Nineteen forty-four would prove to be the Home Guard's last active year of existence. By August it was clear to all but the most die-hard Home Guard supporters that, as the allies had now gained a solid foothold in northwestern Europe, Nazi Germany was no longer capable of launching any kind of invasion of the United Kingdom. That said it still came as a shock to many when on 6th September P J Grigg, the Secretary of State for War, made a radio announcement stating that from that day on Home Guard operational duties were to be suspended and that all parades would be voluntary. A follow up announcement in late October set the date of the stand down as early November.

The War Office decided that to mark the occasion various nationwide events and parades should be organised on Sunday 3rd December by as many Home Guard Battalions as possible, with a central event taking place in London - over 7,000 Home Guards, drawn from units across Britain marched through the West End to Hyde Park where they were reviewed by King George VI, their Colonel-in-Chief, and other leading dignitaries. The Marlborough Battalion sent along a number of representatives including Private Ted Watts from Ramsbury.

In Marlborough special arrangements had been made to transport men from the outlying villages into the town, and at 11am the battalion marched into St Mary's church from various directions filling the building to its limit. After singing the hymns 'All people that on

By 1943 it was beginning to dawn on even the most ardent Home Guard supporter that a German invasion of the United Kingdom was fading with each passing day.

Defence and Home Guard monthly magazine *(top left)*, was full of rousing stories or tips to help boost moral, and the 'Laughs' series of cartoon booklets, which included titles such as 'Laughs on the Home Front' and 'Laughs with the Forces', also produced 'Laughs with the Home Guard' *(top right)* allowing the force an opportunity to smile at itself.

Despite these efforts absenteeism (mainly due to long hours of work in the factories and on the land) was causing concern, as the allied planners needed a strong Home Guard to patrol railway lines during the invasion period.

In April 1944 the 'Mein Pal!' poster *(left)* was released to discourage shirkers, but it did more harm than good, as it appeared to suggest that the whole force was dodging its responsibilities, and was quickly withdrawn.

earth do dwell', 'O God our help in ages past' and 'Onward Christian Soldiers' a short address was given by the vicar of St Mary's, the Reverend Canon Swann.

After leaving the church the battalion formed up and marched into the High Street via London Road with HQs Company in the lead followed by A, B, C and D Companies - more than 800 men in total. Platoon commanders marched at the head of their platoons with second-in-commands bringing up the rear. Leading the entire column was Marlborough's Battalion's Commander, Lt. Col. Walter Giffard. Standing on a platform outside the Royal Oak was General Sir Francis Gathorne Hardy, who took the salute as the column marched past. On his right, dressed in his robes of office, was the town Mayor, Col. C W Hughes, and playing rousing marches in the centre of the street was the Marlborough and Kennet Vale joint band.

After passing the dignitaries the column continued on towards St Peter's church where it wheeled left and left again eventually forming up in the centre of the street facing the saluting base. General Gathorne Hardy then gave a lengthy address, which was followed by more speeches by the Mayor and Lt. Col. Giffard. The day had been cold and overcast and as proceedings began to draw to a close it started to rain! Eventually the Battalion was dismissed for the very last time and as the men headed back to their homes or waiting transport all they had to remind them of their four-and-a-half years of service were the uniforms they stood up in and the vague promise from the government of a medal and certificate of service. However, on the Wednesday following the stand down there was one final chance for everybody to get together again at a farewell social held in the Marlborough College gymnasium - 280 men attended, but this really was the last hurrah.

The 6th Marlborough Battalion, led by Lt. Col. Giffard, marches past the saluting base during its stand down parade on Sunday 3rd December 1944. Taking the salute is General Gathorne-Hardy and standing slightly behind and to his right is the town mayor Col. C W Hughes. (Photograph courtesy Wiltshire and Swindon Record Office. G22/295/1)

## 6th (Marlborough) Battalion
### WILTS HOME GUARD

❧

Battalion Headquarters
## FAREWELL DINNER

❧

29th November, 1944
ROYAL OAK HOTEL

*(signatures)*
S. Philpott Sgt.
E. Gregory Pte.
H. Walton Pte.
C. Lovelock Pte.
J. C. Bundy
H. Edwards
J. W. Herd
Tim Shaw
*(signature)*
W. Boyd
A. H. Stone Sgt.
S. T. Huntley
J. Bennett
E. Smith
H. J. Minns
R. J. Dobson
*(signature)*

---

Lt. M. W. HERD

## PROGRAMME
✳

| | |
|---|---|
| Piano Accordian Selections | Pte. C. Knight |
| Song | Sgt. G. Beasant |
| Monologue | Cpl. H. Mercer |
| Song | Pte. E. J. Newman |
| Piano Selections | Pte. C. Knight |
| Comedy Song | Pte. A. New |
| Monologue | Cpl. H. Mercer |
| Song | Sgt.-Major E. Smith, M.B.E. |

Community Singing

---

**I**n the years when our Country

was in mortal danger

NORMAN JOHN DAY

who served from July 1940 to Dec. 1944

gave generously of his time and

powers to make himself ready

for her defence by force of arms

and with his life if need be.

*George R.I.*

## THE HOME GUARD

---

***Top:*** A farewell dinner was given for members of 6th Battalion HQs on 29th November and this souvenir programme was signed by some of those present. (via G Johnson)

***Above:*** The Defence Medal was awarded to every Home Guard who had served for more than three years.

***Left:*** A certificate of service, like this example given to Norman John Day from Ramsbury, was sent to all who had served in the force.

# 10. Group photographs

Unfortunately, despite requests made throughout the region, via local radio, newspapers, village noticeboards and shop windows, it has been impossible to find photographs for every unit or platoon that formed the 6th (Marlborough) Battalion, Wiltshire Home Guard. However, some platoons had more than one group picture taken, but at different times, and they are also included in this section.

With the passage of more than 70 years, and the loss of so many veterans during that time, it has also been impossible to name every individual in every photograph and in some cases there are many gaps! Nevertheless, despite these shortcomings a large number of group and individual photographs, representing many of the battalion's men and units, are reproduced on the following pages together with as much information as possible. Also slotted in between photographs at appropriate points are stories that were difficult to place in other parts of the book.

If any reader can put names to the faces, correct errors, provide additional photographs, stories or documents the author would be delighted to hear from them and can be contacted via the address given at the beginning of the book.

**Right:** Sidney Gilbert was a member of the East Grafton Platoon and is pictured somewhere in the village wearing his Home Guard uniform. When he first tried to join he was rejected because he was too young, but his older brother Jim, and father Stanley were both in the platoon and he told them, *"If you can hold a rifle, so can I."* His persistence paid off and despite still being under age was eventually accepted. The platoon often went on night duty up on the downs around Wexcombe and slept in tents. To shield himself from drafts Sidney always tried to ensure that someone slept between him and the tent opening. (Mrs Sylvia Gilbert)

# A curious change of name

It was common practice for wartime Home Guard Battalions to have at least one regular serving soldier attached on a permanent basis to act as an instructor. During its four-and-a-half year existence the Marlborough Battalion had several instructors who stayed with the unit for varying periods of time, but the background of Sergeant George Edward Smith is more interesting than most.

He was the son of William Camp, a railway porter, and was born in West Ham, London on 14th October 1912. For some unknown reason when he joined the Wiltshire Regiment in November 1930 he lied about his surname. He wasn't under age, as he had just passed his 18th birthday, so was he trying to escape from something such as an ex-girlfriend, his family or the law?

There is no doubt that Smith and Camp are the same man as his service number (5567971) is the same throughout his army career. The name on the British Empire Medal he received following the grenade incident at the Butts, Marlborough on 7th December 1941 is Smith. However, the General Service Medal he was awarded a few years later is inscribed to Camp!

George Edward Camp retired from the army in 1957 and died 30 years later in Benfleet, Essex. Those members of the Home Guard who knew Camp all remember him as a very good and competent instructor. The above information and the medal group shown below have been kindly supplied by Will Bennett from London. Will was born in Wiltshire and has for many years collected medals associated with the county.

***Above left:*** A 1944 picture of George Edward Smith/Camp

***Left:*** His medal group mounted as worn with the BEM (far left) back to front.

## 'A' Company, 6th (Marlborough) Battalion, Wiltshire Home Guard

*This picture was taken in the gardens of the Priory during 1941 (via John Robins). Names should be read left to right.*

**Back row:** ?, ?, ?, ?, ?, ?, ?, Herbie Dancey, ?, Ernie Pagington, Edwards, Alf Stevens, Jim Ellam, Frank Lovelock, Peter Woodford, ?, ?, ?, ?, ?, ?, ?, Bull, ?, ?, ?, ?

**4th row:** ?, ?, ?, ?, ?, ?, ?, ?, ?, ?, ?, Les Hancock, ?, ?, ?, ?, ?, ?, ?, Alan Newman, ?, ?, Charlie Cully, ?, ?

**3rd row:** ?, ?, ?, ?, ?, ?, Abe Batty, ? Bert Dobie, Jack Wiltshire, ?, ?, ?, ?, Fred Burgess, ?, Ronald Robins, Cannon, ?, ?, ?, Stacey Philpot, ?, Percy Ford, ?, ?

**2nd row:** ?, ?, Fred Witts, Jack Philpot, Tom Lovelock, Percy Hulbert, Bill Foot, ?, Harry Kerr, ?, Siddall, Cook, Parmenter, Col. Christopher Hughes, ?, ?, ?, Jack Pearce, ?, Wilson, ?, Harry Mundy, ?, Sydney Sayers, Nobby Swatton, ?, ?

**Front row:** Tony Pearce, ?, ?, George Langford, Chuck Purton, ?, Ernie Johnson, ?, Doug Green, ?, Mick Matthews, John Bower, Alfie Dobson, Arthur Tarrant, ?, ?, ?, ?, ?, ?, ?, ?, ?

**'A' Company, 6th (Marlborough) Battalion, Wiltshire Home Guard**

*This picture was taken on the steps of the college cricket pavilion during October 1944*

# 'A' Company, 6th (Marlborough) Battalion, Wiltshire Home Guard

*Names should be read from left to right:*

**Back row:** James Duck, Brown, ?, Powell, Sawyer, ?, ?, ?, ?, Ernie Major, ?, ?, ?, ?, Arthur Rossiter

**8th row:** ?, ?, Jack Allen, ?, ?, ?, ?, ?, ?, Cook (chemist), ?, Stan Hillier, Fred Cleverly, ?, ?

**7th row:** ?, Sutton, ?, ?, Bill Roff, Canning, Mundy, ?, 'Win' Spanswick, Bob Gough, ?, Hillier, Dick Milsom, ?, ?

**6th row:** ?, ?, Abe Batty, Jack Rawlings, Bob Bowden, Easter, ?, ?, ?, ?, ?, ?, Arthur Gardner, ?, ?, ?

**5th row:** George Angliss, ?, 'Dicky' Bird, Dunford, Dunford, Peter Woodford, Geoff Sandford, Bert Dobie, ?, Ernie Pope, Sutton, George Johnson, Charles Quarterman, Dick Bull, Herbie Dancey, Stan Milsom

**4th row:** ?, ?, Les Hancock, ?, Newman, Joe Bernard, 'Natto' Dunsby, ?, ?, ?, ?, ?, ?, Alfie Ingram (wooden leg), Collins, ?

**3rd row:** ?, ?, Chapman, ?, Chandler, Jack Stone, Stiles, 'Snowy' Sawyer, ?, Walt Dunford, ?, ?, ?, Mick Mathews, Tom Hawkins, ?, Fred Dobie

**2nd row:** Charles Hughes, Jim Ellam, Eric Free,Jack Wiltshire, Fred Burgess, Wilson, Charles Jennings, 'Nobby' Swatton, Harry Mundy, Garside, ?, Fullerger, Wally Dance, Ronald Robins, William Bower, Cannon, Bill Osgood

**Front row:** Sgt Maj Smith, Maj Shaw, Clay, ?, Bill Foot, Tom Lovelock, Jack Philpott, Sayer, Pearce, J Parmenter, J Siddall, Perkins, Neate, ?, Ernie Newal, Walter Giffard (Battalion Commander), Peter Davies (publisher), ?

## No. 4 Platoon, 'A' Company

**Back row:** ?, ?, ?, ?, ?, ?
*Middle row:* ?, ?, ?, ?, ?, ?
*Front row:* Mick Matthews, Wally Dance, Cannon, Pearce, Ronald Robins, William Bower, ?

## No. 6 Platoon, 'A' Company

*(picture via Mrs Wendy Stevens)*
**Back row:** Hiller, Stan Hillier, Bill Roff, Canning, ?, Bob Gough, Fred Cleverly
*3rd row:* ?, Sutton, ?, ?, ?, 'Win' Spanswick, Arthur Gardner
*2nd row:* ?, ?, ?, ?, Alfie Ingram, ?, ?, ?
*Front row:* ? ,Charlie Jennings, Harry Mundy, J Siddall, Ernie Newell, 'Nobby' Swatton, ?, ?

## No. ? Platoon, 'A' Company

***Back row:*** Peter Woodford, Dunford, 'Dicky' Bird, ?, ?, ?
?, ?, ?, ?, ?, ?, ?
***Front row:*** ?, ?, Eric Free, Tom Lovelock, Jack Philpot, Charles Hughes, Jim Ellam, ?, ?

## Marlborough College B3 LDV Platoon - July 1940

***From left to right:*** John D Jennings, Geoffrey T Rose, Michael W B O'Loughlin, Maughan W Innes,
John S Hattersley, Bryce B Ramsden, John H Hunt, Peter M Castle-Smith, Alan P L Cowan*,
John Anderson, John B Wilson, Geoffrey W Moberley*, David M Summerhayes, Hugh P G Bond.
*Picture taken in Marlborough College grounds (via John Wilson)*
*\* Sadly both these boys were killed in action later in the war.*

**Avebury Platoon, 'B' Company, 6th (Marlborough) Battalion, Wiltshire Home Guard**

*Names to be read from left to right*

***Back row:*** Dennis Blake, ?, Reg Vickers, Tommy Hancock, Reg Kepence, Les Hart, ?, Tom Page, Ellis Cook, Wally Vickers, ?, ?, Jack Rickards, Fred Cable

***Middle row:*** 'Binks' Cottrell, Gordon Blake, Frank Cullis, ?, Jack Sherman, Ernie Hart, Harold Durnford, Les Drew, Dick Humpheries, ?, Bill Blake, Stan Blake, Frank Horsell, ?

***Front row:*** George Stevens, Henry Blake, Pat Stewart, Charles 'CD' Perry, William 'WEV' Young, ? Dick 'Monkey' Brown, Rex Huntley, Percy Blake

*The barn in the background, which was burnt down postwar, was just to the west of Avebury's Great Barn.*

The Avebury Platoon used part of the ditch of the ancient monument to the north of Green Street for shooting practice, which is where both these photographs were taken. The men appear to be armed with a number of US P17 rifles and a couple of Sten guns. (Wiltshire Folk Life Society via The National Trust)

## Beckhampton Platoon, 'B' Company, 6th (Marlborough) Battalion, Wiltshire Home Guard

*Back row:* Murray Davis, Bob Hues, Leslie Harper, Jim White, Bill Greenaway, George Harper, Bill White
*Middle row:* Fred Maslin, Stable Lad, Les Greenaway, George Blake, Fred Nash, Stable Lad, Reg Perry (back), Stable Lad (front), Stable Lad, Bill Vines, Stable Lad, Bill Pictor
*Front row:* Arthur Furniss, Norman Bertie, ? , Fred Darling, Percy Cottrell, Tom Blake, Roger Hues
*The building in the background is part of the racing stable complex at Beckhampton.*

# Beckhampton Platoon

When the platoon was formed, Fred Darling, a well known and successful race horse trainer with stables at Beckhampton, announced that he would be its commanding officer. Second in command was his head travelling lad, Norman Bertie, and the platoon's sergeant was another Beckhampton trainer Herbert Blagrave.

In 1940 Roger Hues was 18 years old and as well as working for his father on a farm in the village was also a corporal in the platoon. He remembers that on Sunday mornings, after the horses had been ridden out, the platoon would meet up in a big room at the stables and parade in the yard. *"Fred Darling was of the old school - he was tough. [One day] I missed a parade and the next time [the parade met] he called me aside and said 'one more time and you're out!' - I'd never been spoken to quite like that before. On another occasion some senior officers arrived and I was in charge [of the parade]. I didn't call the men to attention properly - they said I should have made them jump up and salute - I got another rollicking for that!"*

The following account, which shows just how tough Darling could be, is regularly recalled by local people and has almost assumed folklore status. The platoon was on an exercise one night up on the downs. Darling and a group of senior Home Guard officers paid them a surprise visit and found an OP that should have been commanded by Pat Templeton, Darling's head lad, deserted and the men drinking in a nearby pub. Templeton was sacked 'on the spot' from his job at the stable, dismissed from the platoon and made to vacate his tied home in the village. The shame was too much and soon afterwards he took his life. Despite everything Darling did have some redeeming features, which included buying everyone a pint at the Wagon and Horses after Sunday parades.

On occasions the tedium of lectures and guard duty was enlivened by exercises. *"I remember going into Manton on a big do with the Home Guard"*, recalls Roger Hues. *"We had a lot of rifle practice and were allowed to fire into a hay rick, but it didn't seem to occur to anybody that the rick would catch fire! On the same day a German bomber flew over very low and we could see its black crosses - everybody scattered."*

The 6th June 1942 edition of Picture Post carried an article about Fred Darling and two horses in his care, Big Game (whose picture is on the front cover) and Sun Chariot. They were both owned by the National Stud, but were leased to King George VI and ran in his colours.

**Winterbourne Bassett Platoon, 'B' Company, 6th (Marlborough) Battalion, Wiltshire Home Guard**

*Pictured at a Sunday parade on the green near the church*

From left to right: Sgt. George Fox, Cpl. Bob Haines, Frank Cook, Sammy Hicks, Wally Ricards, Dennis Bridges, Bill Missen, ?, ?, ?, Roland Garrett, ?, ?, ?, Ron Bridges, ?, ?, ?, Sgt. Maj. George Smith. (Picture via Ron Bridges)

# Overton Platoon, 'B' Company, 6th (Marlborough) Battalion, Wiltshire Home Guard

*Seated left to right:* Jack Light, Alex Emberlin, 'Chicko' Southam, Bert Peck, John Durston, ?, George Lanfear.
*Standing:* ? , Bill Deacon or Joby Lanfear, ? , ? , ? , Sgt. Ash, ? , Stan Fry, ? , ?

*Below left:* 2nd Lt. Bert Peck, Overton Platoon's Commanding Officer.
*Below right:* Sgt. Ash (left) and Bert Peck. (All pictures via Audrey Peck)

# Lockeridge Platoon, 'B' Company, 6th (Marlborough) Battalion, Wiltshire Home Guard

Unfortunately the author has been unable to find a group photograph of the Lockeridge Platoon. However, Fred Mundy, who lived with his family at 6 Rhyles Cottages, Lockeridge, was a member of the platoon and these pictures were taken in his garden.

*Above left:* Fred Mundy with his Lee Enfield rifle.

*Above right:* Mum's Army!

*Left:* Fred, Audrey and Lily. (All three images via Audrey Peck)

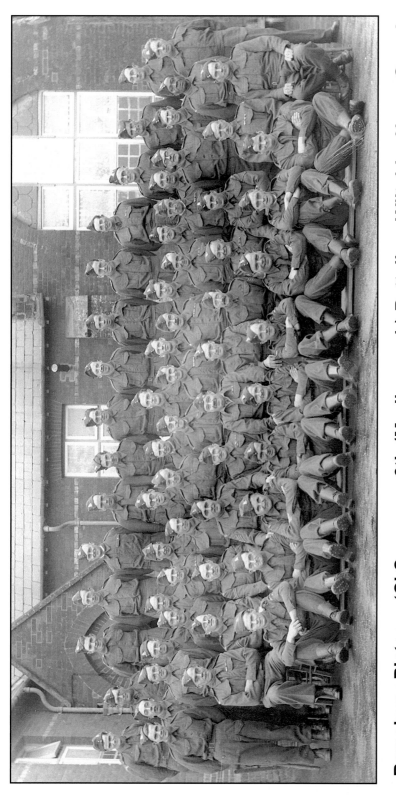

## Ramsbury Platoon, 'C' Company, 6th (Marlborough) Battalion, Wiltshire Home Guard

*Back row:* E Newman, W Chamberlain, R Griffin, Goodship, A Wheeler, Blandford, Griffin, E Hedges, P Westall, J Day, E Martin, Newman, Thomas, E Martin, W Grant

*3rd row:* A Barrett, G Claridge, Talmage, S Mildenhall, Phillips, F Hunter, F Chamberlain, F Wootton, J Isles, J Sheppard, J Dixon, F Hunter, A Exell, E Watts, R Rushen, Williams, M Hughes, A Rosier, ?, F Newman, W Parry, R Lockey, L Palmer, W Dyer, E Barrett, R Dixon

*2nd row:* F Starling, H Palmer, H Davis, G Wilson, S Smith, E Wilson, J Watts, A Pike, T Peck, G Edwards, W Giddings, J Claridge

*Front row:* R Whitbread, G Orchard, Watts, Sheppard, H Watts, D Huntley, Barrett, G Chamberlain, W Chamberlain

*Picture taken in the playground at Ramsbury school*

103

# Aldbourne Platoon, 'C' Company (Marlborough) Battalion, Wiltshire Home Guard

*Pictured in the yard at Manor Farm during 1944*

**Back row:** T. Warner, J. Bomford, T Trotman

**4th row:** D. Barnes, P. Haines, J. Roberts, W. Lee, J. Lee, W. Sheppard, W. Price, H, Aldridge, W. Hargreaves, F. Mildenhall, W 'Pelly' Barnes, A. Palmer, J. Mildenhall, H. Barrett

**3rd row:** J. Morris, E. Avery, J. Wilkins, H. Hamblen, J. Emberline, W. Jerram, J. Cuss, W. Liddiard, S. Holmes, Mr Maskell, G. Wentworth, R. Read, F. Sheppard, F. Sheppard, G. Jerram

**2nd row (seated):** G. Barnes, Mr McHugh, C. Price, G. Dew, W. Liddiard, G. Sudds, Dr. Varville, Maj. W. Brown**, Capt. V. Bland**, C. Brown, D McKeon, F. Barnes, C Manning, G. Woodin, E. Pike

**Front row:** C. Dixon, W. Hale, L. Hawkins, E. Davis, W. Mayes, F. Wilson, W. Tilly, J. Barnes, T. Coles, H. Herring

*\*\* Major Brown was in command of 'C' Company and Captain Bland was Aldbourne's Platoon Commander. Both were retired army officers who lived in Aldbourne and continued using their pre-war ranks in civilian life. During their service with the Home Guard Captain Brown became a Major and Major Bland a Captain, which must have caused some confusion, especially for people who had known them pre-war!*

104

**Top left:** Tommy Lunn, a Sgt. in the Aldbourne Platoon, in uniform with respirator in the alert position and brandishing a .303 Lee Enfield rifle. Based on the style of armband the picture was probably taken late 1940 or early 1941.

**Top right:** This pad, which dates from the very early days of the Home Guard's existence, belonged to Tommy Lunn and was designed to record enemy activity in the event of invasion.

**Below:** Tommy's daughter Maura (and Sammy the cat) surrounded by his weapons of war. On the right is a 1918 model .300 Lewis machine gun. The barrels of these guns were susceptible to over heating and it was recommended that they should be fired in short bursts of no more than 5 rounds. (Both photographs via Murray Maclean)

# Chilton Foliat & Froxfield Platoon, 'C' Company, 6th (Marlborough) Battalion, Wiltshire Home Guard

**Back row:** E Lane, J Dobson, D Povey, S Holmes, O Dobson, J Looker, G Harrison, M Roberts, F Watts, R Copp

**3rd row:** F Pett, A Dixon, F Bartter, A Ball, S Heath, A Cooper, E Williams, A Pike, F Hart, F Wooldridge, D Smith, V Little, A Cannings

**2nd row:** E Little, J Bray, L Hale, L Rosier, J Skinner, Capt. Brown, T Bucknell, F Mundy, T Smith, R Naish, A Smith

**Front row:** H Brooks, J Bucknell, J Watts, F Lambourn, J Povey, R Rolfe, H Denton, S Cannings, ?

*Picture taken at the Old Rectory, Chilton Foliat. The two men wearing civilian clothing on the left had served in the unit for several years, but had been forced to leave because of their age. However, they insisted on being included in the platoon's group photograph.*

Chilton Foliat's 1941 harvest festival service held in the church of St Mary. Taking the service is the Reverend Pelham (his son, Robert, was responsible for creating the famous Pelham Puppets) and the men on the right are members of Chilton Foliat's Home Guard Platoon. It is believed the soldiers sitting in the left hand pews were members of the local searchlight unit. (via Mrs Pat Smith)

## Memories of Chilton Foliat Home Guard by Ray Brooks

Ray Brooks joined the Chilton Foliat LDV Platoon in 1940 at the age of 16. When he enrolled he was given an armband marked 'LDV', but no weapon - later he received a uniform and a Lee Enfield rifle. The platoon had a shepherd's hut observation post near Littlecote Park Farm where they spent the summer nights of 1940 looking out for German parachutists. The platoon's commanding officer was Lt. Jack Skinner - he lived in Riverside Cottage beside the Kennet bridge, and was the local water keeper. Lou Hale had served in the army during WWI and had lost a leg. He was a Corporal in the platoon and lived in a thatched cottage at Skeates Corner.

Ray recalls firing a Spigot Mortar near the rifle range at Chilton Foliat. The target was a piece of corrugated tin which was cleverly wound backwards and forwards using a system of pedals and pulleys. Initially the weapon was very inaccurate until they discovered the sights had been fitted back to front! Once the problem was fixed accuracy improved dramatically. To defend the village the mortar was dug-in on the village side of Kennet bridge facing towards Hungerford. It had four legs and was very low to the ground. The legs had to be pegged in position or the weapon would jump up in the air when fired. A machine gun was positioned in woodland beside the Littlecote Road, also facing towards Hungerford, and a second machine gun was set up along the Leverton Road.

# Baydon Platoon, 'C' Company, 6th (Marlborough) Battalion, Wiltshire Home Guard

Unfortunately, the author has been unable to find a photograph of the Baydon Platoon. However, the following names, recalled by Len Richardson, are some of those who belonged to the unit.

Colonel Board - Platoon Commander, lived at Middle Pond
Sergeant Dawes - Had a wooden leg
Len Ball
Percy Cannings
Rowland Day - Farmer, lived at Finches Farm
Sid Everett
Bill Habgood
Walter Hall
Herb Hawkins
George Read - Dispatch rider
Len Richardson - Lived in Choles Cottage and worked for Dick Radbourne at Bailey Hill Farm
Clem Smith - Owned a shop in the village
Teddy Taylor - Kept the Red Lion pub
Ernie Westall
Ollie Whiteman - Race horse trainer from Russley Park (Officer)

The following are some of Len Richardson's memories of life with the Baydon Platoon. *"During the harvest time you would get home from work at say 9 o'clock in the evening, change into your khaki uniform, go on guard [all night] and get back at 6am. Then you would have your breakfast, change back into your working clothes and go back out into the harvest fields again.*

*Our HQs was the Methodist chapel [now Chapel Cottage] and we would go there every Sunday morning for instruction. Sometimes someone from the army would come along and teach you how to use a rifle - I could have told him a thing or to! One day we were standing around him in a circle when one of our lot, a well educated fellow, said 'I'd like to know how to load my rifle'. I was standing with my mate Ernie Westall and I said, 'If he's going to bugger about with that rifle let's get behind him'. He had the rifle pointed down instead of up in the air. 'Bang' it went, and the bullet hit the road and shot up in the air - he could have killed somebody!*

*They would inspect your rifle every time you went on parade. You would take the bolt out and put your thumb in the bottom of the breach and the Sergeant would look down the barrel. If it shone up you were alright, but if it was dirty then God help you! I remember going on duty with Teddy Taylor who kept the pub. As we were walking along Ermin Street I looked at Teddy and said 'Where's your rifle?' 'I don't carry that' he said, 'I wouldn't know how to shoot the damn thing if I had it!' We were supposed to have a gas mask, leather belt, bayonet, rifle and five rounds of ammunition when we went on duty.*

*When you were out [at night] you always knew a German aircraft because the plane's engines went burr, burr, burr, but our planes kept an even tone. I was up at Bailey's [Hill Farm] with Percy Cannings and a German plane flew along low by Botley [copse]. Percy had a gun and he trained his gun on the plane. I shouted, 'For Christ's sake don't shoot because he'll turn his machine guns on us and blow us off the face of this earth'."*

# Little Bedwyn Platoon, 'D' Company, 6th (Marlborough) Battalion, Wiltshire Home Guard

Bill Mundy, Frank Keen, Bert Sainsbury, Ernie Luker, Stan Bolland, Joe Waters, ?, George Myall
George Pike, Len Pearce, Billy Webb, Ray Mundy, George Batchelor, Ron Head, Arthur Martin, Arthur Mills, Peter King
Maurice Martin, Bill Mead, John Wildash, William Gauntlett, Arthur Pavey, Bill Harris, Arthur Tarry

*Picture taken at Manor Farm House, Little Bedwyn*

# Great Bedwyn Platoon, 'D' Company (Marlborough) Battalion, Wiltshire Home Guard

*Pictured during 1941 near Great Bedwyn's British Legion Club. Despite the image's early date the platoon is surprisingly well equipped and clearly proud of its two 1918 model .300 Lewis Machine Guns.*

*Back row:* Alf Parker, Charlie Broad, George Tandy, Reg Bowley, Jack Lovelock, Stan Rosier, Les Davis, Arthur Kempster, Vic West, Haines Edwards, Sid Dowton

*3rd row:* Vic Heaver, Ben Lloyd, George Hawkins, Les Wilmot, ? Frazer, Bill Gigg, Bill Killick, John Wilkins, Putty Little, Dan Kerr

*2nd row:* Bill Dines, Norman Tosh, Ned Wild, Joe Davis, Captain D. Paget-Cooke, ? Hylton, Vi Bennett, ? Hands, George Cranstone

*Front row:* Ernie Brown, Ted Mills, Bert Davis, Reg Cope

# Great Bedwyn Platoon, 'D' Company (Marlborough) Battalion, Wiltshire Home Guard

*Pictured during 1944 outside Great Bedwyn's British Legion Club*
*Back row:* ?, ?, ?, Gideon Butler, Les Lawrence, Les Wilmot, Reg Coward, Reg Bowley, Alf Parker, Les Brooks
*3rd row:* ?, Dennis Alderman, George Hawkins, John Wilkins, George Cranstone, Mr Hilton*,
Rev 'Tulip' Phillips, Bert Davis, Reg Cope, Sid Downton, ?, Gordon Edwards
*2nd row:* ?, Ned Wild, Teddy Mills, Vi Bennett, ?, Captain D. Paget-Cooke, Joe Davis, Haines Edwards,
Vic Eaver, Charles Tandy, ?
*Front row:* Ray Holmes, Albert Dines, ?, Arthur Farley, Dicky Bint, ?, Albert Beckenham, ?, ?

*\*Mr Hilton was a naturalised Austrian who had been resident in the UK for many years.*
*Unfortunately, because of his nationality he was forbidden from wearing a British uniform.*

## Shalbourne Platoon, 'D' Company, 6th (Marlborough) Battalion, Wiltshire Home Guard

Bob Waters, Watts, Charlie Tucker, Stan Tucker, Fred Tucker
Wilf Waters, Stan Heath, Henry Dance, Harry Dowdell, Dick Tucker, Fred Waters, ?, Percy Follon, Charlie Stout
?, Bill Allen, ?, Ted Coward, John Couling, ?, ?, Les Follon, Alec Walter, Cyril Walter
Bill Withers, ?, Stan Walter, Percy Walter, ?, Lt. T Burgess DCM, Lt. R C Green, Charlie Strange, ?, ?, ?, Vic Withers
Norman Bird, John Quirk, John Robinson
*Picture taken near the Kingston Room, Shalbourne*

3 Platoon (Shalbourne) Home Guard

D Company

6th Wilts Battalion

_ COPE.

*Above left:* A Shalbourne Platoon compliment card.
*Above right:* Mrs Walter from Shalbourne wearing her husband's Home Guard side cap. (via Mrs Kathy Withers)

## Ham and Buttermere Platoon, 'D' Company, 6th (Marlborough) Battalion, Wiltshire Home Guard

No photograph of the Ham and Buttermere platoon has been discovered. However the following names (extracted from a document held in the county record office, Chippenham, dated about 1941-42) are some of the unit's members.

**Ham Section:** Lt S Brown, K A Bowley, C Myall, N Turner, W Louth, G Mills, S G Cornah, Sgt. Dawes, Pollden, Cpl. J Bowley, L Cummins, Sgt. F F Hill, T Newman, Munn, D Giles, Sgt. F Giles
**Buttermere Section:** Sgt Harriott, Griffin, Wilkins, Whitlock, A Barrow, L Hearne, S Hearne, D Creaton.
*The platoon's commanding officer was Lt. C Macpherson and its headquarters was at Ham Manor.*

## Savernake Platoon, 'D' Company, 6th (Marlborough) Battalion, Wiltshire Home Guard

Originally called Durley Platoon but later renamed Savernake. No photograph has been found, but the following are some of its members.
The Marquis of Ailesbury - Commanding Officer, Lionel Wootton - Sergeant, Mr Ratcliffe, Mr Hale, 'Arty' Stroud, Bill Crook, two Whitbread brothers, George Cady, Ray Beasley and 'Dickie' Brown.

The following memories of the platoon are recalled by 'Dickie' Brown. *"We lived in a half-tiled house in Durley and my job was junior solicitor to Bernard Ford, whose office was in Marlborough. Bernard Ford was also the Burbage Home Guard Platoon's Commanding Officer - we were great friends. Unfortunately he had a weak heart, which caused him to breath heavily. When Savernake Platoon had an exercise against Burbage they* [the men] *used to say, 'Let's hope Bernard Ford is in charge', - they always knew where the* [Burbage] *platoon was, because they could hear him breathing - it was a standing joke!"*

# Wilton and East Grafton Platoon, 'D' Company, 6th (Marlborough) Battalion, Wiltshire Home Guard

*Pictured in front of East Grafton village hall during 1944*

**Back row:** Arthur Drewitt, Jim Gilbert, Ronnie Ricks, ?, Ernie Martin, Arthur Fox, Arthur Elkins, Jimmy Hawkins, Len Hedges, Wilfie Elkins, Ronnie Cox

**Middle row:** Sidney Gilbert, George Bayley, Leonard Wells, Frank Hilliard, Fred Stagg, Benny Hosier, William Eastmond Sr, William Eastmond Jr, Jim Fisher, Joe Webb

**Front row:** Mr Scamell, Stanley Gilbert, Alec Rebbick, Fred Rosier, Dick Margesson, Col. Snow*, William Mundy, David Lemon, Billy Litten, Tom Wolford, Charlie Hayward

* Col. Snow was 'D' Company commander, but lived at Wilton, which is presumably why he is in this group.

# Gazetteer

The following is a list of some of the known defensive positions that formed part of the Marlborough anti-tank island, together with their six-figure OS 1:25,000 grid reference.

| Location | Defensive work | Grid reference | Status |
|---|---|---|---|
| Herd Steet | Roadblock | SU 190694 | Removed |
| Junc Blowhorn St/St. Martins | Strongpoint | SU191694 | Removed |
| St. Martins | Roadblock | SU191693 | Removed |
| The Green | Type 25 pillbox | SU190693 | Removed |
| Junc Silverless St/Herd St | Type 24? pillbox | SU190693 | Removed |
| Silverless Street | Type 25 pillbox | SU189693 | Removed |
| Kingsbury Street | Roadblock | SU187691 | Removed |
| Kingsbury Street | Pilbox, type uncertain | SU187691 | Extant |
| Junc Silverless St/Kingsbury St | Strongpoint | SU187691 | Extant |
| London Road | Pillbox, type uncertain | SU191691 | Removed |
| Lane by Castle & Ball | Roadblock | SU186691 | Removed |
| Hyde Lane | Roadblock | SU186689 | Removed |
| Sun public house | Type 25 pillbox | SU185688 | Removed |
| Wykeham House | Type 25? pillbox | SU186688 | Removed |
| St Peter's Church A4 | Roadblock | SU186688 | Removed |
| St Peter's Church Lane | Roadblock | SU186688 | Removed |
| Mount House | Strongpoint | SU185688 | Removed |
| College arch | Roadblock | SU184688 | Removed |
| Pewsey Road | Roadblock | SU186687 | Removed |
| Cowbridge | Roadblock | SU187686 | Removed |
| Cowbridge | Type 24 pillbox | SU187686 | Extant |
| George Lane west | Roadblock | SU191689 | Removed |
| George Lane east | Roadblock | SU192689 | Removed |
| Kennet Bridge A4 | Roadblock | SU192690 | Removed |
| West of Roebuck Inn | Roadblock | SU195691 | Removed |
| Railway bridge A4 | Roadblock | SU201689 | Removed |
| Railway bridge A4 | Pillbox (25) north A4 | SU201689 | Removed |
| Railway bridge A4 | Pillbox (25) south A4 | SU201689 | Removed |
| Railway bridge A4 | Railblock | SU201689 | Unknown |
| Track to old signal box | Roadblock | SU194685 | Removed |
| Railway bridge A346 | Roadblock | SU194685 | Removed |
| Old railway goods yard | Railblock | SU192685 | Removed |

# Bibliography

Listed below are books and magazines that I have referred to during my research. To their authors I offer my sincere thanks.

*609 at War,* by James Douglas Earnshaw (Vector Fine Arts, 2009)
*Dad's Army,* by David Carroll (Sutton Publishing, 2002)
*Don't Panic,* by Mark Rowe (The History Press, 2010)
*From Dusk till Dawn,* by A G Street (George G Harrap, 1943)
*Guns, Kites and Horses,* by Sydney Giffard (The Radcliffe Press, 2003)
*In the Space of a Single Day,* Jon Mills and Terry Carney (Wardens Publishing, 2001)
*Insane and Unseemly,* by John Saville (Matador, 2009)
*Ironside's Line,* by Colin Alexander (Historic Military Press, 1998)
*Home Guard Humour* (Amberley Publishing, 2010)
*Home Guard List 1941 - Southern Command* (Savannah Publications)
*Paths of Progress,* by Thomas Hinde (James and James, 1992)
*Pillboxes,* by Henry Wills (Leo Cooper, 1985)
*Ramsbury at War,* by Roger Day (Privately published, 2004)
*Savernake at War,* by Roger Day (Privately published, 2007)
*Stand Down,* by L B Whittaker (Ray Westlake Military Books, 1990)
*The Battle of Britain, Then and Now,* by Winston G Ramsey, 1980)
*The History of the Wiltshire Home Guard,* by E A MacKay (Wiltshire County Territorial Association, 1946)
*The Home Front,* by Peter Doyle and Paul Evans (The Crowood Press, 2007)
*The Home Guard,* by David Carroll (Sutton Publishing, 1999)
*The Home Guard,* by S P MacKenzie (Oxford University Press, 1995)
*The Home Guard,* by Neil R Storey (Shire Publications, 2009)
*The Home Guard of Britain,* by Charles Graves (Hutchinson, 1943)
*The Real Dad's Army,* by Norman Longmate (Hutchinson Library Services, 1974)
*The Somerset Home Guard,* by Jeffrey Wilson (Millstream Books, 2004)
*To the Last Round,* by Austin J Ruddy (Breedon Books Publishing, 2007)
*Uniforms of the Home Guard,* by Richard Hunt (Historic Military Press, 2002)
*Vehicles of the Home Guard,* by Martin F Mace (Historic Military Press, 2001)
*Wings over Wiltshire,* by Rod Priddle (ALD Design and Print, 2003)
*Within the Island Fortress - No. 2 Identity Cards, Permits and Passes,* by Jon Mills (Wardens Publishing 2006)

## Magazines
*Britain at War magazine,* various issues

## Unpublished documents
*The William Young Diaries,* Wiltshire Heritage Museum Archive and Library, Devizes